Response to *Oxen*

"Most of the time we tend to blame our circumstances for our situation rather than choosing to overcome them! In this book Joe Sangl shows us not only that overcoming our financial circumstances is within our reach, but he also shows us how to do it. I must warn you, after you read this book you will no longer have an excuse to remain in financial bondage."
-- **Perry Noble**, author *Unleash!*, founding pastor of NewSpring Church, www.PerryNoble.com

"Joe Sangl is a powerful communicator who has lived the message of this book personally. From both the Bible and his own experience, he clearly and practically shows the way to living a more abundant life with our faith, money and dreams. *Oxen* provides the resources we desperately need to embrace a life of personal and financial freedom."
-- **Jud Wilhite**, author of *Torn*, senior pastor of Central Christian Church, www.centralonline.tv

"As a pastor I have noticed there are some communicators who possess a "golden hammer" that can tap a scripture and it fall into magnificent pieces of truth. What Joe Sangl does with Proverbs 14:4 is nothing short of remarkable in deriving truth after truth, precept after precept and principle after principle. His financial principles from this one Proverb will revolutionize a person's financial life if he or she will simply follow the outline. I have been blessed to hear Joe present this material twice in person and each time I have walked away with a greater appreciation of the verse and the truths that Joe revealed. I am a raving fan of Joe Sangl and an even bigger fan of making sure I've got oxen in my stalls!"
-- **Dr. Dwight "Ike" Reighard**, author and leadership expert, President/CEO of MUST Ministries, senior pastor of Piedmont Church

"Joe Sangl is passionate about helping people accomplish their dreams - and God's dream - for their lives. *Oxen* will help countless people realize those dreams. In an engaging, personal, and easily accessible style, *Oxen* shows you how to get paid whether you are working or not. Not only will that help families realize their dreams, but it will release more funds than ever before for ministry through increased generosity. As a pastor and church leader, that excites me greatly. I will be personally recommending this book to many, many people."
-- **Carey Nieuwhof**, lead pastor of Connexus Church and author of *Leading Change Without Losing It* and co-author of *Parenting Beyond Your Capacity*

"A few years ago I had the privilege of introducing Joe Sangl to West Ridge Church. His time with us was a financial game changer for so many of our people. I love Joe's heart and his contagious enthusiasm to help people accomplish far more than they ever thought possible. I believe the principles found in *Oxen* could revolutionize the way you manage your financial world."
-- **Brian Bloye**, senior pastor of West Ridge Church and president of The Launch Network

"Joseph Sangl's *Oxen* reveals the biblical blueprint for maximizing financial resources. I believe every person who reads it will have a transformed view of money and the power of oxen. You will be equipped to achieve an abundant harvest."
-- **Tony Morgan**, author, leadership coach and consultant, www.TonyMorganLive.com

"I've known Joe Sangl for many years and this is his best work. The reason I love this book is Joe helps the everyday person understand how they can live their dreams. The next level of your financial future depends on how many oxen you have. This concept is revolutionizing how I look at the world and freeing my family up for the future we desire. This book will help you accomplish far more than you ever thought possible in your life!"
-- **Casey Graham**, entrepreneur, founder of The Rocket Companies, www.CaseyGraham.com

OXEN

The KEY to an Abundant Harvest

JOSEPH SANGL

NIN Publishing

OXEN
Published in the United States by NIN PUBLISHING – Anderson, SC

This book was written to provide accurate information on the subject matter covered. Please be advised that Joseph Sangl is not engaged in rendering legal, financial, accounting, tax, or any other professional advice. Before making any decisions regarding your own personal or business financial situation, you should first seek the advice of a proven and competent professional.

Printed in the United States of America
Signature Book Printing, www.sbpbooks.com

Cover design by Ken Wilson – www.avclub.us
Edited by Rachel Rivers

Library of Congress Control Number: 2012914598

Sangl, Joseph

ISBN 978-0-615-68206-8

First Edition

To my bride, Jennifer;

My daughter, Melea;

And my son, Keaton.

And to every person whom I have had the privilege of meeting along the way.

"Where there are no oxen, the manger is empty, but from the strength of an ox comes an abundant harvest."

– Proverbs 14:4 –

Contents

INTRODUCTION

It is my personal calling and passion *to help people accomplish far more than they ever thought possible*. In my travels around the world teaching personal finances, I have discovered that most people have a huge dream that seems out of reach due to its tremendous financial cost. The amount of money required just to take a beginning step is so high it becomes unachievable. When faced with such tremendous financial challenges, many people resort to making statements like, "I will have to win the lottery to accomplish my dream."

The facts are clear. Most people struggle financially. Every single month, all of their earnings come in only to be immediately sent back out to pay the bills. The few dollars they do manage to keep seem to be apprehended by unanticipated large expenses. This cycle of working hard to earn money but never being able to get ahead can leave one feeling nearly hopeless – like abundance and financial freedom are just not possible.

Even more than the tremendous financial costs, many people are completely intimidated by the hard work required to achieve their goal. Most have no idea where to even begin learning how to do the work necessary to fund it. They have no example of anyone who has actually prospered financially within their own family or circle of friends, and most schools don't provide strong teaching on the subject. As a result, most people start believing the lie that they cannot win with money and then they stop dreaming.

This does not have to be the case for you! I promise you that this book will help you reap an abundant harvest that can be used to fund your personal dreams and those you have for your family and others. You will be equipped to think differently about what you currently do have and how you utilize your existing and future resources. It is my hope to help you transform a mindset of "Where can I spend this money?" to "How can this money be utilized to fund my dreams so huge that I can't even bring myself to speak them out loud?" and to move your actual financial situation from a position of "I have very little" to "I am living the abundant life!"

When you finish this book, it is my hope that you will have experienced the following:

- A changed view of the world
- A changed view of your resources
- A mindset shift from "empty manger" living to "abundant harvest" thriving
- An acceptance of the challenge to acquire oxen
- A new understanding of money that has equipped you to acquire, manage, and lead oxen
- Inspiration to take action!

Everything written in this book is not simply a theory. Countless others have used this wisdom to prosper. It is what I have personally done, and I know it works. Even more importantly, YOU can do this!

1

Proverbs 14:4

Where there are no oxen, the manger is empty, but from the strength of an ox comes an abundant harvest. Proverbs 14:4 (NIV:1984)

I will never forget the day I first read Proverbs 14:4 in my Bible. My family had embarked on a journey to become financially free, and I was reading the entire book of Proverbs to find verses providing wisdom about money and money management. Many verses in Proverbs were already well-known to me and had made a profound impact upon my life. Proverbs 22:7 (*The rich rule over the poor, and the borrower is servant to the lender*) motivated me to pursue debt freedom. Proverbs 13:22 (*A good man leaves an inheritance for his children's children …*) challenged me to think generationally, ensuring I leave a financial legacy, so I could position my descendants to prosper.

Proverbs 14:4 never registered on my radar until that day. Its wisdom gripped me and stopped me in my tracks. *Where there are no oxen, the manger is empty, but from the strength of an ox comes an abundant harvest.* I read several Bible translations for this verse to ensure I fully understood its message.

- *Where there are no oxen, the manger is empty, but from the strength of an ox comes an abundant harvest.* (NIV:1984)
- *Where there are no oxen, the manger is empty, but from the strength of an ox come abundant harvests.* (NIV:2010)
- *Where no oxen are, the crib is clean: but much increase is by the strength of the ox.* (KJV)
- *Where no oxen are, the manger is clean, but much revenue comes by the strength of the ox.* (NKJV)
- *Where there are no oxen, the manger is clean, but abundant crops come by the strength of the ox.* (ESV)

- *Where no oxen are, the manger is clean, but much revenue comes by the strength of the ox.* (NASB)

I grew up on a small farm. We raised or grew just about anything and everything. We had pigs, cows, ducks, and chickens. Our crops included corn, soybeans, wheat, and hay. I loved growing up on a farm. It is where I learned the value of hard work, about sowing and reaping, the cycle of life, and how everything in God's creation is interconnected and dependent upon each other.

Maybe Proverbs 14:4 connected with me so strongly because it was talking about a life I knew that included farm animals, farm equipment, and a harvest, but I think the real reason it connected with me is because it described my financial situation - my manger was empty.

As I describe in my book *I Was Broke. Now I'm Not.*, I was the youngest of six boys, but I was the first to graduate from college with a bachelor's degree in mechanical engineering from Purdue University. Because of an amazing employer that had a college tuition reimbursement program, I was able to further my formal education and obtained a master's degree in business administration from Clemson University. My career had moved rapidly upward and so had my salary, but even with all of these tremendous blessings, I was broke. Every single dollar I earned was deposited into our bank account, but all of it was delivered to one of our many debts or to pay bills by the end of that very same day.

My manger was empty.

I don't know if you have ever watched cattle eat from their mangers, but they will stand eating at a manger until all of the food is gone, and then they will lick the manger clean just to ensure all remaining scraps are consumed. This described my financial situation. I could scrape together enough money to pay the bills, but beyond that there was absolutely nothing left over. Every single spare dime we gained inevitably departed our presence – never to be seen again. Our version of "licking the manger" was running out of money and then physically turning our piggy bank over to find enough coins to buy food off the dollar menu.

The same scenario played out every single month. We made money, and then we consumed every last dollar. Just like the oxen, we would be faced with an empty manger and were forced to stand around waiting for the next paycheck to refill it. It seemed like there was never enough for the moment, let alone storing up for the future.

On the day I encountered Proverbs 14:4, I realized that the writer shares two potential outcomes: an "empty manger" and an "abundant harvest".

Two Potential Outcomes – Proverbs 14:4
1. An empty manger
2. An abundant harvest

If you were given the choice of an "empty manger" or an "abundant harvest," which outcome would you choose? I may never have the privilege of personally meeting you, but I do know one thing about you: If given the choice, you would select an "abundant harvest" over "empty manger" every single time.

An empty manger is barren. It represents hunger and potential famine. The manger once held food, but now it is cleaned out. It has nothing left over. To more fully comprehend this, imagine that your entire house is void of food – the pantry, cupboards, and refrigerator are completely empty.

An abundant harvest is presented as an alternative outcome. I liked the sound of this much better than an empty manger. An abundant harvest suggests that we have a full manger – all of the time. Dictionary.com defines "abundant" as *"present in great quantity; more than adequate; oversufficient."*

As I pondered these two potential outcomes. I sensed a life-changing moment approaching. I knew if I could truly grasp the wisdom contained within this verse, my life would be radically changed. As I read the verse again, I saw what made the difference between an empty manger and an abundant harvest: oxen.

Read the verse again. What leads to an empty manger? No oxen!

Look at the verse again. What leads to an abundant harvest? Oxen!

It was at that very moment I realized the choice was up to me. I could live with an empty manger or with an abundance. It made so much sense. I am confident my upbringing on a farm helped me gain this understanding. You see, it is immediately obvious to a farmer that he must have oxen to produce an abundant harvest. A farmer would never attempt to do his work without oxen – whether they are real oxen like the Amish still use or modern-day oxen like John Deere tractors.

Imagine a farmer who was responsible for farming a full section of 640 acres, which is one square mile of land. Imagine if he decided to "do it all on his own" and attempt to plow all the ground without oxen. It doesn't matter how strong and energetic the farmer is, it would be an impossible task. For me, just hoeing a small garden in my back yard wears me out! The farmer might be able to do enough work to produce food for the family to eat, but the potential for an abundant harvest would be impossible.

Don't miss the point here because it is vital to understanding oxen ownership. A farmer **knows** it is **impossible** to reap an abundant harvest without oxen. The same is true for all of us even if we aren't farmers.

If I continued managing my money without the help of financial oxen, the opportunity for an abundant harvest would be greatly limited. After all, there was only so much I could accomplish on my own. Like most people, I was working a "Work, get paid. Don't work, don't get paid." job. Even if I worked twelve hours every day, there was a limit to how much I could earn on my own. My earnings would allow me to feed my family, but without a serious change to the way we managed our money, the income would probably only be enough to maintain our household. We would continue to be stuck in the "empty manger" cycle cleaning out the manger each month and then standing around waiting for the next paycheck to arrive. The worst realization of all was knowing that even if I worked for fifty years of my life, my income would cease the moment I chose to retire. It became imminently clear that I needed oxen in order for my family to experience abundance.

With this new revelation and life-revolutionizing understanding, I embarked on a journey to find and acquire oxen. I talked to anyone who would listen and several who would not. I pondered it day and night. In fact, I talked so much about Proverbs 14:4 that my mother even wrote it down on a small dry erase board she keeps on the refrigerator. It has remained written there for over ten years. Every time I visit my parents, it is a constant reminder that this teaching must be shared with others.

There is a choice each person must make. In pursuit of financial abundance, you can choose to rely on yourself and your own abilities, or you can acquire oxen to help you. Don't miss my wording here. It is a *choice*, whether a conscious one or not, that each one of us will make as we journey through life.

I have chosen to acquire oxen, and have found Proverbs 14:4 to be absolutely true. While my family's oxen acquisition journey has been adventurous, frightening, incredible, and exciting, I have discovered that the strength of oxen has indeed led to an abundant harvest. The same can be true for you. All you need is some good oxen.

Now I have one question for you:

Got oxen?

2

Types of Oxen

With all of this talk about oxen, it would be helpful to understand "oxen" in our present day situations. The definition of an "ox" for the purpose of this book is as follows:

OX *n.* Any resource that enables people to accomplish far more than they could on their own.

Note that in Proverbs 14:4, the word "oxen" is plural: "where there are no oxen, the manger is empty." This means it is important to have more than one ox. Think about it. If you have only one ox and it dies, you will immediately face an "empty manger" again. If you have multiple oxen, the loss of an ox will be painful, but it won't immediately lead to a situation where you are solely reliant upon yourself to produce an abundant harvest.

There are almost unlimited varieties of modern-day oxen that can help you produce an abundant harvest, and it is important to possess several types. In investing terms, this is called *diversification*. Dictionary.com defines "diversified" as "distributed among or producing several types." The Bible refers to the importance of diversification as well. Ecclesiastes 11:2 shares this wisdom: *"Give portions to seven, yes to eight, for you do not know what disaster may come upon the land."* Diversification allows you to continue to produce an abundant harvest even when some oxen falter.

With the importance of oxen and diversification in mind, let's review many common forms of oxen that people possess.

Company Stocks If you own a company stock, you actually own a portion of that particular company. This means you are entitled to a portion of the profits as company leadership chooses to share them with its shareholders. Additionally, the value of the company could increase and increase the stock value. A herd of this type of oxen can yield an abundant harvest over time.

Consider the following two questions:

1. As a shareholder, do you work for the profits the company produces?
2. Do the company's employees work to produce profits even while you are sleeping?

The answer to #1 is "No", and the answer to #2 is "Yes." You don't work for the profits the company produces – the employees of the company do! In other words, the money you paid for stock ownership is literally working for you. Your **ox** works for you even while you are sleeping. That is awesome!

Do you see the oxen concept more clearly now? A company stock is a modern-day ox, multiplying your efforts far beyond what you could do on your own. Of course, company stocks can behave much like young and strong oxen sometimes do – running around in a frenzied pattern because of their incredible energy. Company stocks can change in value quite rapidly at times. This is why it is important to have a diversified set of oxen.

Apple, Inc., the computer and mobile electronics company founded by Steve Jobs, Steve Wozniak, and Ronald Gerald Wayne in 1976, made its first public stock offering on December 12, 1980.[i] An initial share of stock sold for $22.00. As of the printing of this book that one share of stock would now be worth more than $3,600 – an increase of 16,455%.[ii] Not too shabby of an ox to have working for you!

Bonds A bond is a debt owed by a company or other entity. While borrowing agreements can vary, here is a common way that a bond works: In exchange for your money, the borrower agrees to pay an established amount of interest payments for a set period of time. Once this time passes, the company returns all of the borrowed money to the lender. Bonds are issued by the federal government, companies, municipalities, schools, and churches as they seek to raise money for various projects or initiatives.

Again, consider the following two questions shared in the company stocks section. Do you work for the interest paid to you? Absolutely not. Your ox (the bond issuer) does. Again this is a situation where interest payments are produced even while you sleep! It bears repeating – oxen allow you to accomplish more than you could on your own.

In general, bonds are calmer than stock investments. They are similar to a mature ox that is fully trained and is no longer given to wildly bounding around a field. They are generally reliable and focus on accomplishing the task before them.

Mutual Funds & Exchange Traded Funds (ETFs) Acquiring oxen one at a time can be quite time consuming and costly. Mutual funds and ETFs allow you to acquire herds of oxen with a single purchase. Mutual funds and ETFs are financial oxen that are funded "mutually" by investors like you, me, and 3,000,000 of our closest friends. Each person invests a different amount. Fund managers pool this money together into one very large account, and use it to make investments into a wide variety of companies.

As this "herd of oxen" yields profitable growth, the investment value increases. Mutual Funds and ETFs have specific charters that guide the actions of the fund managers. For instance, one mutual fund might focus solely on established companies in the United States while another invests solely in up-and-coming companies located in third world countries. ETFs might have a charter to invest only in the thirty companies that comprise the Dow Jones Industrial Average (DJIA) or the Standard & Poor's 500 (S&P 500).

Retirement Plans - 401(k), 403(b), 457, TSP, 529, IRA, Roth IRA, Simple IRA, SEP, RSP, or Pension Plan Retirement plans allow people to purchase a variety of oxen: stocks, bonds, mutual funds, and ETFs. By themselves, these oxen can carry huge loads and produce a tremendous harvest, but most retirement accounts provide another distinct advantage – tax savings! In ordinary retirement accounts, the government allows you to retain the income taxes owed and invest that money as well. This can allow you to increase your herd of oxen more rapidly. Once the money is withdrawn for use during retirement, taxes become due.

Other retirement accounts such as the Roth IRA allow you to invest money that has already been taxed, but allow the account to grow completely free of taxation. Upon retirement, the money remains free of taxation.

Most employer-provided retirement accounts offer another distinct benefit – a company match! For example, one company allows their employees to contribute up to fifteen percent of their income to their 401(k) account. For the first three percent of income contributed to the retirement account by the employee, the company will match that contribution with another three percent. In other words, if an employee invests three percent of their income into the 401(k), the company will match it with a 100 percent return on investment **automatically** and **without risk**!

Real Estate – Residential, Commercial, and Land Real estate can be a huge ox. While it can be quite costly, it can yield some of the greatest harvests. Suppose a single-family house is purchased with the intent of renting it to someone else. The home is purchased for $100,000 and leased for $800 per month. If rent is actually paid each month for a year, the total rent collected would be $9,600. Maintenance, insurance, taxes, and miscellaneous expenses of $4,600 are paid which means there was $5,000 profit for the year. This is an immediate financial return of five percent on investment. However, one must also take into account the value of the home. Suppose the value increases by two percent each year. This would be a net worth increase of another $2,000 (two percent increase on the initial home value of $100,000). This means that the overall increase for the year is $7,000 (seven percent).

This type of investment generally requires more active involvement than a stock, bond, or mutual fund investment, but many people have discovered this to be a very enjoyable ox to own.

Money Market Deposit Accounts, Savings Accounts, and CDs These types of accounts are generally very calm oxen. They usually provide a specific rate of return in exchange for the use of your money. The bank utilizes your money as one of their oxen to lend to some poor soul on a 19.99 percent credit card. In return for the use of your money, the bank gives a small portion back to you. This type of ox is reliable, but it also does not have the ability to carry much of a load. It is highly unusual for the interest paid on this type of account to even keep pace with inflation.

Antiques Many people have generated wealth from old and nostalgic items. You and I might see something that is rusty and needs to be thrown away, but that very item might be worth thousands of dollars to a collector. If you know the business, antiques can yield a tremendous return on investment. This market can be highly volatile based upon the availability of each item and the whims of consumers. It is also susceptible to decline when the economy falters and people have less money to spend on these items.

Precious Metals Gold, silver, platinum, copper, and nickel can produce wealth. While the markets for these metals tend to fluctuate wildly at times, many people have generated substantial profits through well-timed investments. A common reason given for investing in precious metals is that this type of currency has been around far longer than any other type of currency including the United States dollar.

Talents I've discovered that there really is no better investment than investing in a true talent or ability that you possess. If you are a great singer, you could invest in producing an album. If you have a gift for making people laugh, you could be a professional comedian. If you love to write, write a book or freelance magazine articles. If you are blessed with creative ability and love gardening, become a landscape designer.

Identify something you do very well and enjoy. If you are really good, there is a chance you could produce income while living out your passion. This is the best type of ox of all!

I wrote the book, *I Was Broke. Now I'm Not.*, so I could provide a resource to people searching for a way to win with their personal finances. This ox has given me so much joy as I have seen it carry a message of financial hope around the globe, and it has enabled me to pursue my true passion in life – helping people!

Inventions or Intellectual Property Inventions and intellectual property can have incredible value and can produce a hugely abundant harvest. In the fall of 1993, a dental student named Rich Bailey showed up at a Missouri State University football game in Springfield, MO with what appeared to be a terrible case of buck teeth, but they were actually false teeth. Jonah White, an entrepreneur in the making, was greatly humored by the teeth and met Rich after the game. Jonah discovered that Rich had made the terrible set of false teeth as a joke while being taught how to make dentures at dental school. The rest is history. The Billy Bob Teeth Company was founded and has manufactured over 20 million sets of teeth and has sold them in over 95 percent of the countries on earth.[iii] Their invention has yielded an abundant harvest plus a lot of laughs!

Perhaps you possess a patent or other intellectual property that could be licensed to another company. That ox could generate an abundant harvest for you with absolutely no future effort required!

Small Businesses – Your Own or Investment Into Those of Others
Successful small business owners find a need in the world and fulfill it. Small business opportunities are almost limitless. A short trip down the

main street of any town or city will allow one to see dozens if not hundreds of small businesses in action. You could start a business from scratch, buy an existing business, acquire a proven franchise, or even invest in another person's small business dream.

Either way, I have discovered this to be true: if you are blessed as an individual, you can bless many, but if you are blessed with a successful business, you can bless multitudes!

Your Current and Future Jobs It would be a shame to mention all of these types of oxen without including your current and future jobs. After all, a job is the catalyst that will provide the very funds used to acquire additional oxen. There are many people who despise their job and are constantly frustrated by any number of grievances they have with their employer. Resist the temptation to do this yourself. My recommendation is to steer clear of these types of people, and focus on the fact that your employer provides the ability to produce income you can use to acquire oxen!

Leaders If you are the leader of any organization, you know the burden of carrying the mantle of leadership. All of the decisions seem to flow to and through you. You are faced with a barrage of questions on a daily basis. If you attempt to carry this burden alone, you will end up exhausted and burned out by the very mission that used to be your passion. This is why you need leaders that can help shoulder the load for you! You can certainly accomplish something great on your own, but so much more can be done with the help of leaders who help you carry out the mission and vision.

These are just a few examples of oxen that you can possess. Just remember that there are literally millions of oxen you could choose, and each one can help you fund your dreams. At this point, don't focus too much on the type of oxen you currently own or that you might seek to acquire. For now, it is most important for you to understand that oxen are *the key* to an *abundant harvest*.

3

What Oxen Can Do for You

Oxen are highly versatile, and you must understand all their capabilities in order to maximize their potential. First and foremost, it is important to know that oxen can allow you to earn money regardless of whether or not you are working.

To better understand this, it is really important to examine the two ways income is generated.

Two Key Ways to Earn Income

Income Earning Method #1	Income Earning Method #2
Work = Get Paid Money AND Don't Work = Don't Get Paid Money	Get paid whether or not you are working!

Method #1 is the most common way people earn money. They work for money. Nearly everyone has done this. For example, I worked at a race horse farm as a teenager. I cleaned stalls, mowed grass, and helped train foals. In return for my effort, I was paid money. If I did not show up to work, I was not paid. This is the most basic way people acquire money, and it is the only way many people have ever known.

Method #2 is also a common way for people to earn money, but for some reason, far less use this approach. It is a method commonly referred to as "making your money work for you." One example is owning a McDonald's restaurant franchise. Many times when driving home from a speaking event, I am lured into a McDonald's drive-thru by the thought of a delicious double cheeseburger and an ice cold Coke®. Who receives the profit from my purchase? Is it the person working the drive-thru? Absolutely not. The drive-thru operator is earning money using Method #1. The person that keeps the profit is the franchise owner who is using Method #2. Even though the owner is asleep at home, she is making money! Method #2 is employed by most wealthy people, and it is the very reason they have achieved their wealth.

If you have a choice (and you do) between Method #1 or #2, Method #2 is better because there is only so much you personally can do. We are all limited to just 24 hours each day. Method #2 allows you to eliminate the time barrier altogether by leveraging the efforts of many people who work on your behalf.

Oxen Can Do Things You Cannot Do. Oxen are huge animals, often weighing in at 2,000 pounds or more. They are rippling with muscles and have tremendous strength – far more strength than any human could ever hope to have. It is from this very strength that an abundant harvest can be gained. An ox has four legs which provides it more pulling power than your two legs ever could. The beast can withstand weather of all types: hot, cold, rain, and snow.

When you obtain a financial ox such as a 401(k) investment account, it will do things you could never do your own. It will provide unbelievable power to fund your dreams. Ultimately, it can help you withstand all sorts of financial storms: an economic downturn, a job loss, or an illness.

Oxen Can Carry a Load You Cannot Carry. Let's face it. There is only so much weight you can bear. This is why most people have empty mangers. They carry a huge financial load that their regular income cannot support. Despite their best efforts, the financial load continues to grow. Their children need braces and college expenses continue to approach. An illness or injury is experienced, and along with the frustrations of the situation is the financial load of having to pay for a huge insurance deductible.

Financial oxen can carry huge loads for you. A financial ox allows you to transfer some of the load from your regular income onto its back.

Suppose you have a profitable small business you operate in addition to your regular job. Those earnings can help cover some expenses and reduce the burden on your regular income. When this happens, it sets the stage for an abundant harvest. Are you beginning to see how oxen can help you carry a huge load? It is simply amazing!

Oxen Can Endure More Than You Can Endure. An ox can endure tremendous extremes. It can thrive even when faced with harsh weather conditions or labor demands. Its strength and design allow it to handle far more than you or I ever could. God created it for a reason: to bear tremendous burdens and accomplish difficult work.

If you have the right financial oxen, they will endure far more than you could individually. Which of the following two options for income production would you choose when faced with a financial obstacle?

- A. Your lone source of income produced from your daily job
- B. Your income from your daily job PLUS profits from a small business PLUS a growing retirement account PLUS a profitable rental real estate investment

Obviously Option B would be the best scenario because your financial oxen are able to bear far more than you could on your own.

This raises a very important point. Consider the two situations outlined in Options A and B again, and suppose the financial obstacle you faced was the loss of your job. In Option A, your job is the lone source of income, so income production is now reduced to zero. Let's look at the two options for income production now that a job loss has occurred:

- A. NONE
- B. Profits from a small business PLUS a growing retirement account PLUS a profitable rental real estate investment

Do you see it? By obtaining oxen, a person can free themselves from being totally beholden to their employer for financial survival. Incredible!

Oxen Can Be Trained. Oxen are domesticated animals and can be trained to do many tasks. They can pull various tools such as plows or harrows. They can pull a wagon. The animals can be trained to walk in circles, along straight lines, or to just stand still. Once an ox has been trained well, it needs little to no guidance. The animal can almost operate on its own. Many farmers who have used oxen to plow fields can vouch for this very fact. Their oxen know the task so well that they will turn around at the end of the field on their own and head back down the field in perfect alignment with the next furrow to be plowed.

Your financial ox can be trained too. Suppose you have started a small business. From the very first day you start it, you train it to operate in the way you want it to work. This includes designing systems and processes that guide the business, as well as providing ongoing training for every employee. Once the course is set and focused training has taken place, it can operate with far less of your energy and guidance.

Oxen Can Work Together to Accomplish Even More. The Bible speaks specifically about the power of working together. The writer in Ecclesiastes 4:9-12 shares how two are better than one and finishes the script with the amazing statement that, *"A cord of three strands is not quickly broken."*

I'm told that one ox can pull a tremendous load, but two oxen working together can pull exponentially more than each could pull on its own. This is a significant fact to understand when acquiring financial oxen. If careful attention is given toward the selection of your oxen, you can find some that work well together. When this happens, greater things can be achieved.

For example, suppose you owned a profitable retail business. The business grows and requires retail space, so a location is rented in a four unit commercial building. Knowing the power of multiple oxen, you begin to store up profits while renting that one retail space. Eventually, you can utilize those profits to purchase the entire commercial building. This allows you to have two oxen: a retail business and the four unit commercial building. Working together, these two oxen can do so much more than the retail business could on its own!

Your retail business ox produces profit which allows you to acquire the four unit commercial building ox. Of course, your retail business must continue to pay its monthly rental expense, but this expense is now transferred directly to your new ox – the commercial building. You are taking money from one pocket and putting it into another instead of handing the money to someone else.

This creates a win-win-win (what I call a triple win) situation for you:

1. Your small retail business wins because its location is now permanently secured.
2. Your commercial building business wins because it now has one space permanently leased.
3. The overall profits end up in your pocket instead of someone else's.

It is a wonderful situation to have oxen working together. By joining the forces of your oxen, amazing things can be accomplished!

Oxen Will Work Rain or Shine – Night or Day. An ox does not really care what the weather is; it is equipped to work in virtually any condition. Its strength and power allow it to plow through mud. Its tough hide allows it to take a beating without injury. It will work night or day.

This is the case for a mutual fund ox. If the mutual fund owns stock in companies that operate around the globe, you will literally make money while you are sleeping. Suppose one of the stocks owned within your mutual fund is a company located in Japan. While you slumber, the fine people working in the Japanese companies are hard at work delivering profits for you. What a great ox!

Oxen Can Take You Places. Oxen can be trained to fit a harness which allows them to pull a wagon. This means they can pull you anywhere. It might take awhile because of their slow speed, but there is no doubt they will get you to your destination.

Financial oxen will take you places too! The resources received by using oxen will allow you to give extravagantly, bless your family, travel extensively, and fund dreams you never thought possible.

Oxen Can Multiply. Two oxen of the right types can produce baby oxen! In financial terms, if you have some successful businesses, they can produce such an abundant harvest that they are able to fund the birth of another business! This is where the harvest can grow ridiculously large.

Consider this thought. If two oxen birth a baby ox, who feeds the baby? You or the mother ox? The mother ox! This is a vital point, and please don't miss it. If one of your oxen give birth to a baby, the ox that gave birth will fund the baby ox – not your personal income!

One of my brothers started a lollipop sales company when he was in elementary school. He used money earned from his job working for our father to purchase lollipops. He bought the suckers for a few pennies at the store and then sold them to his classmates at school for five to fifty times the original price. It was highly lucrative, and this ox began to carry a load for him. He could have used the profits to birth a bubblegum business. If he had made this decision, the lollipop business would have paid for the start up costs of the bubblegum business, not earnings from his job. Do you see it? The parent ox (the lollipop business) would fund the baby ox (the bubblegum business).

My brother was on his way to becoming a mogul, but our mother caught on to what was happening and stopped it. In other words, she killed his ox. This happens sometimes. Oxen die. Undaunted by this loss, my brother went on to become an incredible salesperson (surprise!) and obtained many oxen that have helped him carry a huge load.

Oxen Can Provide Food and Supplies. An ox can be food for you. It provides milk which can be used for producing butter, cheese, and a variety of dairy products. You can also eat the oxen! Since an ox must be slaughtered to eat it, leather can be made out of its hide.

From a financial sense, this is what occurs during retirement years. Some of the acquired oxen must be consumed. A retirement account is an example of this very thing. The ox is birthed when the 401(k) is started. It is nourished with contributions, and over time it grows into quite a herd of oxen. At retirement, the 401(k) is killed and consumption begins.

Now that you know what oxen can do for you, you surely see the importance of owning some of them. It will not happen overnight, but with diligence it can. If you are currently locked in a Method #1 "Work, get paid. Don't work, don't get paid." manner of producing income, resolve to immediately begin saving money so you can purchase oxen. After all, oxen are the key to experiencing an abundant harvest.

4

What Oxen Can Not Do for You

I am sure that by now you are already considering the potential oxen you are going to obtain, but before we move forward, it is important to understand some things that oxen simply cannot do.

Oxen Cannot Be Productive All by Themselves – They Require Training, Guidance, and Leadership! Oxen require leadership. An ox will not walk out of the barn and straight into a yoke and harness all by itself. That would be strange indeed. An ox must be led to the yoke and fastened into a harness. It must be guided through the work. If you believe you can own oxen without it requiring any of your attention, you are in for a big surprise!

Oxen must be continuously trained. If you are birthing an ox, you have the advantage of training it from the very beginning. You can incorporate key principles you want the ox to represent. If you purchase an ox, you might have to retrain it.

Once oxen are obtained, many people make the mistake of believing that they have "arrived" and begin to cease doing the very things that led to their success. Usually there are no short term effects caused by "taking a break", but if you take too long of a break, the effects eventually arrive with severe consequences. I call this the "ceiling fan effect". Even though you turn off the switch to a ceiling fan, it will continue to spin for a little while. Without flipping the switch back to the ON position to again provide energy to the fan, it will stop turning.

I witnessed this at a business I assisted in reviving. The owner had "unplugged" from the leadership role entirely. The business continued to operate profitably for awhile, but eventually it lost its way, profits disappeared, and losses mounted. In other words, the energy source for the business was gone for too long; the fan stopped spinning. The ox nearly died, but the owner re-engaged and provided leadership and guidance again; the light switch was turned back on. The business was restored to profitability once again.

Take a look at any financial ox you have observed. I guarantee you the ones that have been truly successful for the long-term have an engaged leadership team that provides ongoing guidance, training, and equipping. Conduct a detailed autopsy on financial oxen that you have seen die, and you will find that many of them had little to no leadership involvement.

Oxen Cannot Magically Appear Out of Thin Air. Many people without oxen are waiting for one to magically arrive. This will not happen. They might as well believe in unicorns. Each of my businesses occurred as the result of focused and intense effort.

In the days when nearly every person was involved in agriculture in some way, this was an obvious fact. A farmer could wish all day long for an abundant harvest to appear, but nothing would happen without doing the work to till soil, plant seed, pull weeds and harvest crops.

This is a lottery mindset, and it is ridiculous. It is what I call a "hope so" mentality. Many people operate in a fairy-tale land where they believe that "good things will come to those who wait." I once worked with a leader who shared the following statement that addresses this mindset so well: *"Things come to those who wait, but only things left behind by those who hustle."*

If you have fallen into this trap (and we have all done so at one time or another), today is the day that you end it. Stop hoping to win the lottery or for a million dollar inheritance from a long-lost relative. Instead, focus your energy on doing the work necessary to build up your own herd of oxen.

After all, it takes God Himself, time, money, energy, and patience to obtain, train, and lead oxen. You will experience stiff competition, labor issues, lackluster customer response, and financial challenges. It is part of the process. Be prepared to work very hard to acquire or birth your oxen.

Ask any person who has started a business if it just magically happened. I once heard financial guru Dave Ramsey share an interesting encounter he experienced. After Dave secured a position on the Fox Business Network, he was asked how it felt to be an overnight success. Dave's reply was incredible: "It's taken me 19 years of hard work to become an overnight success!"

Oxen Cannot Do the Work Only You Can Do. While possessing an ox is a terrific thing, it is important to recognize that you will still be required to do the work that only you can do. An ox cannot provide strategic thinking or leadership. It cannot prepare a detailed step-by-step written plan. Do not approach oxen acquisition as a way to completely cease being a productive individual with a ticket to sit on a beach somewhere and waste away the remaining years of your life.

A leader of a non-profit charity wondered why his organization was struggling so mightily to raise the funds necessary to operate at peak efficiency. The results from their work were incredible. Volunteers and employees executed their duties flawlessly. The ox was producing a harvest, but it was unable to produce enough money to keep it alive. The problem was solved when it became clear the leader had failed to do one simple task: ASKING people to donate to the very worthy cause! The ox could not ask for money; the leadership had to. The requests were made, and the amazing charity is now fully funded.

Oxen Will Not Change Who You Are; They Will Only Amplify Who You Already Are. Many people believe they would be different "if they were rich," but money only magnifies who you really are. I hear many people say they would be very generous if they were rich, but they aren't giving any money away in their current circumstance. Their lack of generosity will not change much even if they gain substantial resources. On the other hand, if one currently lives a life of generosity, that person will also be very generous when they gain an abundant harvest.

Since I love people and seek to help them win with their lives, at times I have been guilty of trying to change them. I have discovered that I simply cannot do it. God changes people. I have begged, pleaded, threatened, and challenged people to change, but ultimately each individual must make changes for themselves with His help. If you know there is an area of your life you do not want to have amplified by the abundant harvest you are preparing to receive, reach out and ask Him to help you change. He is faithful to hear and help you!

5

Why So Few People Have Oxen

As you pursue the acquisition of oxen or focus on birthing an ox, you will realize how few people actually have oxen. Most people survive solely on the income produced by their job. As a result, their ability to prosper is entirely dependent upon their ability to work. There are many reasons why people do not possess oxen, and it is important to understand these reasons because you will surely face similar obstacles in your own journey to transfer your financial burdens.

Oxen Cost Money to Acquire. Oxen are not free. If you want to transfer your burden to an ox, you must first spend money to acquire one! Suppose the ox you are pursuing is a Subway® franchise. When faced with the franchise cost, it can stop a person's pursuit of oxen altogether. You have certainly heard the old adage that "it takes money to make money." While this is true, it can take far less money than one might initially think.

Many never even consider what life might look like if they had a few oxen working upon their behalf because most people live paycheck to paycheck. They have zero financial margin. As a result, they can't even fathom spending money on an ox. People who are living financially broken lives tend to only look at the next five or ten days and hope they can survive them. If you have financial margin you can think in increments of five and ten years!

Oxen Cost Money to Maintain. The costs do not end with the acquisition of an ox – it's where they begin! After acquiring the ox, you must feed it, provide facilities for it, maintain its harness and yoke, and treat it when it falls ill.

If you purchase a manufacturing company, you will have to pay for employees and their benefits, repair the roof, and mow the grass. Money will have to be spent on research and development, equipment, and marketing.

Your ox will cost you money to maintain, no matter how profitable it is. The pressure created by this ongoing maintenance cost causes some people to refuse to acquire any oxen at all.

I have learned to embrace these costs. In fact, I refer to each of these costs as "investments." I genuinely believe the money spent to pay employees is an investment that will generate a financial return not possible without them.

Oxen Require Direction and Guidance. Oxen need leadership. Left alone, they will stand around eating and sleeping all day long. To be fully productive, oxen must be placed into the yoke and harness and led to their work. Initially, you might be the only person who provides direction to your business, but as your herd grows, you can hire people who can help lighten your workload in this area.

While some are blessed with the natural gift of leadership, most leaders develop their leadership skills over time and make plenty of mistakes along the way. Many people feel intimidated about being a leader. They feel that they have never led anything in their life, let alone a business. The great news is that you can learn to become a leader. It is okay if you are fearful of being "the man" or "the woman" with all the answers. Take time to develop your skills, and you can become a great leader.

Oxen Ownership Involves Risk. Oxen have been known to die. Many people have heard the horror story of the person who started a business that subsequently failed and caused them to declare bankruptcy. When you acquire an ox, it might fail even though you have prayed fervently and conducted thorough due diligence. The rental house you purchase might have a cracked foundation and termites may chew up the walls. Your business may encounter stiff competitive challenges that eliminate all profits.

It's risky to own oxen, but I believe it is more risky to never own oxen. If all I have are my own two hands to produce a harvest, I am limited to what I can accomplish alone. It is as if I have put all of my eggs into one basket. What would happen if I fall ill or am injured? What will happen once I am no longer able to work and produce income? There will be no oxen to carry the load for me and my family. I will be solely reliant upon Social Security, a system known to be broken by anyone who can do basic math. I decided it is more risky to "go it alone" than to take on the challenge to manage and acquire oxen!

Everywhere you turn, you can find someone who is telling you about all of challenges of the economy and just how crazy it is to deal with oxen. They will point to current circumstances and use them as justification to do nothing. It was on the day I first read Proverbs 14:4 I realized I had been listening to people who had never owned oxen. Even more, they were not experiencing an abundant harvest for themselves! In other words, I was obtaining financial advice from broke people. No wonder I was broke! I tuned these non-oxen owners out and sought out advice from people who were experiencing an abundant harvest.

To be clear, there will *always* be some level of risk – either of taking action or taking no action at all. Embrace it. Pray for God's guidance. Seek wisdom from knowledgeable people. By following God's leading and having wise counsel around you, you will be able to confidently take the steps you know you need to take, even when they seem frightening and perilous.

They Have Never Learned the Power of Oxen Ownership. Many people never acquire oxen because they are not aware of the possibilities that come with owning oxen. Perhaps they have never known anyone who owned an ox. Maybe they have been working so hard they never considered an alternate way to make money. They have not taken the time to consider what could happen if they chose to work smarter, not harder.

It felt as if scales fell from my eyes when I realized the power of Proverbs 14:4. With each ox I have owned, I have observed its strength and become more fully convinced it is the only way I can achieve an abundant harvest.

They Do Not Believe It Is Possible for Them to Own Oxen. Some people do not have oxen because they simply believe it is not possible for them. They will make a statement such as, "I know they were able to do this, but my situation is so much different than theirs," or they will say, "Sure, it worked for them. They started out life way better off than I did." They genuinely believe it is not possible for them to own oxen. Within their sphere of influence they have never seen anyone prosper. There are no tangible examples of accomplishment. I call this "broke thinking."

This broken thought process can be summed up with two single words – "no hope." Lack of hope can make the heart sick and completely blind people to the opportunities and potential that is right before their very eyes. In order to own oxen, a person must first believe it is indeed possible. Faith and belief are foundational to the achievement of any dream.

Do you believe you can own oxen and experience an abundant harvest? Do you *really* believe it? I ask the question twice because without faith and belief, it will make this process nearly impossible. Belief provides the fuel you will need to stay the course.

6

Prepare for Oxen Ownership

There is no one "perfect and right" way, but there are some essential components that maximize your efforts to obtain oxen. As you read each section of this chapter, I challenge you to rate yourself from 1 (Poor) to 10 (Excellent) on how you are currently doing with each component.

1. *Develop a Plan for Your Life*

Why do you want to have oxen? I believe your answer will surely include "to fund a dream," but apart from that your answer may not be easy or straight forward. If you are going to embark on this quest to own oxen, it is important to understand why you are doing this in the first place!

Have you ever taken the time to write your hopes, plans, and dreams down on paper? During our Financial Learning Experience live events, in which our team equips people to win with their personal finances, we have surveyed our audiences and discovered that nearly half of the participants have never in their adult lives taken the time to write their dreams down on paper! Is it any wonder so many people are frustrated and wandering through life? It is tough to achieve anything great even when we have a written and detailed plan, but it becomes impossible without any written goals!

Before you read another page, I challenge you to dream for the next ten minutes. Write your goals in the space provided. Here are some starter statements and questions to help you.

- What are the hopes, plans, and dreams I have for my life?"
- Where do I want to travel?

- I want to give money to …
- What do I want to provide for my children?
- What type of business would I like to own?
- It is my lifelong dream to …

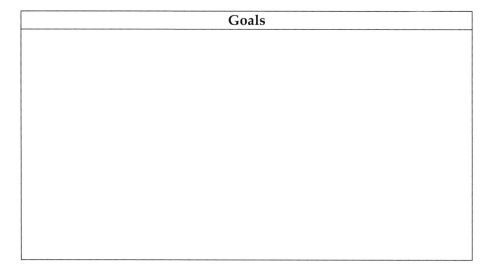

Goals

Look at each of the items you have just written down. Will it require something beyond the income from your regular job to fund them? My bet is that your answer is "Yes."

This is why it is important to have oxen! There might be difficult work involved in pursuing your dreams, but when you see your hopes realized, it will be clear that the effort to gain oxen was worth it. Oxen will help carry the enormous load of making your dreams become reality.

To provide yourself encouragement along the way, be sure to include a line item titled "oxen ownership" in your monthly budget so you can see regular progress toward the funding of your goals.

Rate Yourself
"Develop a Plan for Your Life"

1	2	3	4	5	6	7	8	9	10

2. *Personally Prepare and Live by a Budget*

It is impossible to build anything great without a plan. Proverbs 21:5 says, *"The plans of the diligent lead to profit; as surely as haste leads to poverty."* If you want to have oxen that produce a profit, it is vitally important to learn how to budget. A budget allows you to maximize every single dollar you are blessed with. The act of preparing a plan for your money every single month **before** the month begins is like physical exercise. The more you do it, the better you will become at it. Regular physical exercise improves your health and yields tremendous long-term benefits. The same is true for your finances. The better you become at preparing and living by a detailed budget, the more financially fit you will be to purchase oxen.

The plans of the diligent lead to profit; as surely as haste leads to poverty.
Proverbs 21:5 (NIV:1984)

Proverbs 21:5 provides tremendous guidance. In this verse, we are presented with two outcomes: profit or poverty. More importantly, the writer shares two specific things we can all do to ensure profit is achieved.

Two Things Required to Achieve Profit

1. Have a PLAN
2. Be DILIGENT in following the plan

Your budget is the plan that can point you to profit, but diligence in following that plan is what will ensure the profit is actually achieved!

In my book, *I Was Broke. Now I'm Not.*, I share the vitally important role my monthly budget played in enabling my family to become financially free. At the time I wrote that book, my family had prepared and followed a monthly budget every single month since July 2003. Guess what? This streak has continued forward to this very day because my bride and I know our monthly budgeting process is THE REASON we have been able to even consider oxen ownership! There will never be a month that my bride and I skip the budgeting exercise. It has been that instrumental to our success.

I have heard a lot of reasons people give for not budgeting. Here are just a few:

- "It's too hard."
- "I have varying income, so I have no idea how much I will make this month."
- "My spouse won't work with me."
- "It's too confusing."
- "I just don't have time."

All of these statements have some merit, but they are excuses. I used to make them too. I started winning with money when I stopped justifying my poor money decisions and took the actions required to change my situation. It became even more important when I realized that I was not the owner of my money – God was. Psalm 24:1 shares, *"The earth is the Lord's, and everything in it, the world, and all who live in it."* Since everything belongs to God, including money, it is my responsibility to maximize it for Him! When I considered that I was ridiculously telling God "it is too hard to budget" the money He had blessed me with, it became very easy for me to lay aside the excuses.

Prepare your budget and choose to be diligent in following it. Besides, if you think preparing a budget for your own household is difficult, just wait until you have to manage the budgets of your oxen!

Rate Yourself
"Prepare and Live by a Budget"

1	2	3	4	5	6	7	8	9	10

3. Seek God's Wisdom

I have met many people facing desperate situations with their ox. Their ox is dead or is near death. The reasons for the situations vary greatly. Perhaps they overburdened it with too much debt or excessive salaries. Maybe they purchased an ox that was sick to begin with – believing they could restore it to health. Maybe the market experienced a dramatic shift away from the product or service being provided. It is during these times that I hear people make rather ridiculous statements. They say, "I've tried everything else. All I can do now is pray." This is completely backwards! Prayer is a tremendous idea in times of great trouble, but it is also extremely effective prior to encountering difficulties. Many terrible situations can be avoided altogether when we seek God first!

Throughout God's Word, we are constantly reminded that God is with us and hears our prayers. If we seek Him, we **will** find Him through prayer and reading the Bible. The book of Proverbs is a great place to begin gaining biblical wisdom. Proverbs is full of incredible knowledge that is immediately applicable to oxen ownership.

As a starting point, begin with these verses that have been very beneficial to me.

- Proverbs 21:5, Luke 14:28-30 (importance of having a plan and following it)
- Proverbs 15:22 (importance of mentors)
- Proverbs 13:22, Proverbs 22:6 (importance of thinking generationally)
- Proverbs 13:11 (importance of investing consistently)
- Proverbs 22:7, Romans 13:8, II Kings 4:1-7 (perils of too much debt)
- Proverbs 10:4, Proverbs 6:6-11 (importance of diligence)
- Genesis 41:25-27, Nehemiah 1-4 (importance of margin)
- Romans 12:1-2 (discovering God's will for your life)

Of course, prayer and reading the Word does not guarantee every ox will be wildly successful, but it does mean your steps will be God-led, positioning you in the direct center of His will for your life.

Rate Yourself
"Seek God's Wisdom"

1	2	3	4	5	6	7	8	9	10

4. *Seek Godly Wisdom*

Proverbs 15:22 states, *"Plans fail for lack of counsel, but with many advisers they succeed."* Simply put, this means you need to have mentors and coaches in your life. Of course you can attempt to do anything on your own, but why would anyone want to do that when they could obtain incredible wisdom from people who have already accomplished something similar? If you want to start a car repair business, having a mentor who has already started and operated the same type of business with success would be invaluable! Look at any great team in the world of sports. None of them achieved greatness without a coach. Even superstars in individual sports such as golf or tennis have mentors and coaches and readily give credit to them when they win.

As you embark on your oxen ownership journey, find people who have achieved success and ask them to mentor you. They will be able to provide incredible counsel to you.

Before rushing out to ask someone to coach you, it is wise to establish a set of required qualifications that your mentors must possess. Here are a few characteristics I look for in a mentor:

- *They love Jesus.* I want to know that they are operating from the same playbook as I am.
- *They have no vested interest in my overall success.* In other words, they are interested in helping me be successful, but they are not

going to focus on taking money from my pocket and putting it into their pocket.

- *They have time to mentor me.* I do not drive my mentors crazy with endless requests for meetings and advice, but I do want to know they are available to help me when I am preparing to make a major decision.
- *They have been successful themselves.* I really want to "talk shop" instead of theory. I read books and take classes to understand theories. Mentors help me understand how they have practically applied the theory within their own businesses.
- *They have survived tough periods in their businesses.* During great economic times, it becomes easy for many people to make excellent money. I want to learn from people who have prospered in both good and bad economies.
- *They keep our conversations confidential.* The very nature of our conversation is confidential. If I can't trust someone to keep the conversation quiet, then a great business idea or opportunity could be lost.
- *They have the highest integrity.* The individual must be of the highest character. I want to know that my mentors live a life of honesty and conduct business fairly.

Take a moment to think about the people you believe could really help you as a mentor. Write the name of each person who comes to mind on the chart provided and evaluate them against the key characteristics provided. You might even want to add a few characteristics of your own to this list.

Potential Mentor Evaluation

	Mentor	Mentor	Mentor	Mentor	Mentor
Loves Jesus					
No vested interest in my business					
Time available					
Successful					
Survived tough times					
Confidentiality					
Integrity					
Other:					
Other:					
Other:					

The individuals who have provided godly wisdom to me have had a profound impact on my life. They are THE REASON our oxen acquisitions and births have been viable and successful. Their advice has helped me avoid terrible blunders and also identify additional opportunities I had not previously considered.

Rate Yourself
"Seek Godly Wisdom"

1	2	3	4	5	6	7	8	9	10

5. *Establish Substantial Financial Margin for Your Household*

Whether you are birthing an ox or purchasing one, strive to grow your savings account. This is necessary because most businesses will require cash to purchase or start them, and they will also require additional money to fund the initial operating expenses. A real baby ox faces this actual situation. Before it can carry a load for you, it will require food, shelter, vaccinations, training and time to grow. All these items require money.

Suppose the ox you choose to bring to life is a book. While the book is still a baby ox, you will need to spend money on editing, type-setting, cover art, copyrighting, registrations, and printing. Then after all the time and money spent on these efforts, you will need to spend money to market and sell the book. Unless you are the rare person who has already established a substantially large platform and can command an upfront signing fee from a huge publisher, all this money will be required before you even collect a single dollar from the sale of your first book! Without substantial financial margin, the very life of your baby ox is jeopardized.

It makes no sense to immediately place a newborn ox into a yoke and demand that it begin working. This very idea is preposterous, yet this is the exact mistake many people make when they birth their ox! They birth a business and immediately require it to carry the load of a full-time salary (or salaries). If that burden wasn't enough, credit card debt, small business loans, and maxed out vendor credit limits are added to the load. The baby business ox is crushed before it ever had a chance to mature!

By establishing financial margin from the outset, you will be able to let your baby ox grow up, so it can pull a huge load for you.

Personal financial margin allows you to accommodate surprise expenses your ox may incur. After all, things happen, and it will cost money to address them.

Take for instance a real story that occurred with my father's rental house. The renter, who apparently did not value the house as much as my father, mistreated the house by punching a hole in the wall and destroying the carpet. Each of these events cost money. Another family of renters cleaned out the fireplace and placed the hot coals in a cardboard box. They added to their mistake by setting the highly flammable cardboard box of hot coals on the floor **inside** the house and proceeded to leave the house. The not-so-surprising result was a house fire. Because my father had financial margin in place along with appropriate insurance, the house could be rebuilt. If saving had not been a priority for my father, this situation could have led to an empty manger instead of the abundant harvest the rental home provided over the long term.

If you already have a few oxen, make it your goal to establish enough financial margin so the process of birthing or acquiring another ox will not jeopardize the ability of your other oxen to perform well. In other words, you do not want to overburden your other oxen with all the financial costs of the new one. You can, of course, use some of the financial margin available within your other businesses to fund some of the start-up costs, but the goal is for the other businesses to continue to prosper.

There are two types of personal financial margin:

1. Reserves Margin (money already in savings)
2. Monthly Margin (ability to save money every month)

A savings account filled with money (financial reserves) is wonderful, but birthing an ox without having monthly financial margin can be perilous. For example, an existing savings account balance might be used to make the down payment on a rental home, but how will repairs to the rental be made if there is no ongoing monthly margin? You best position yourself to prosper when you have both types of personal financial margin.

I have a friend who purchases businesses as a hobby. He has established two rules for any business that he purchases. Rule one is that he must be able to pay for the business in five years or less. His second rule is that he must be able to pay for the business with his existing savings and his regular income. In other words, he wants to avoid overloading the newly acquired business with debt payments. This set of rules has served my friend well as he is now a multimillionaire with virtually zero debt. His oxen are indeed carrying a load he could never carry on his own, and they have made many of his dreams become reality.

There is plenty of biblical basis for the importance of establishing margin. Margin covers time of famine. In Genesis 41, Joseph heard Pharaoh's dream and correctly interpreted that there would be seven years of plenty followed by seven years of disastrous famine. Joseph led an effort to store up vast amounts of grain during the time of abundance to ensure the famine would not ruin Egypt. Egypt saved diligently and protected their nation and surrounding nations from perishing.

Margin provides security. Chapters one through four of Nehemiah chronicles the story of rebuilding the wall around Jerusalem. Jerusalem was living in abject poverty because their gates had been burned with fire and their walls were torn down. Without the protection of their city wall, or margin, they were subject to constant raids from the enemy and stranded in poverty. With Nehemiah's strong leadership, the wall was rebuilt in just 52 days, and the city was again able to prosper. I believe that if a wall was built around an entire city in just 52 days, you can build a wall of financial margin in the same period of time.

While it is certainly possible to gain oxen without possessing financial margin, I promise you that strong financial margin will make the journey so much easier and less stressful!

Rate Yourself
"Establish Substantial Financial Margin for Your Household"

1	2	3	4	5	6	7	8	9	10

6. *Establish Substantial Financial Margin for Your Oxen*

It is important that you establish financial margin to allow your ox to prosper. It is miserable to operate any business without cash on hand.

Without financial reserves, an incredible amount of effort is lost balancing bills and making payments. I operate with the philosophy that it is a very rare situation where any business should "bet the farm" and spend every last dime of their money.

If you are starting a new business, it is great to have the "start-up" money saved, so you can focus all of your energy on the new ox without overburdening it with debt and salaries. If you do not have substantial financial margin, however, try to avoid taking a salary at the beginning. This allows all revenue generated to be reinvested into developing the products and services you want to deliver. Many people have successfully started their business "on the side" by continuing to work another full-time paying position.

I have received significant pushback from people who don't want to have a divided focus. They protest, "If I have to start this up as a side job, I won't be able to focus full-time on what I am most passionate about." They are rightly concerned about how exhausted they will become by working a full-time job while also starting up their business. I completely understand this, but starting the business up on the side gives it the best chance to become a full-grown ox.

This is exactly how my first business was launched. I wrote my first book, *I Was Broke. Now I'm Not.*, while I worked a full-time job. I also began seeking speaking opportunities at the same time. Because I was not reliant upon the fledgling business for income, I was able to use all the revenue generated from book sales and speaking to produce additional books, web sites, and resources. It took 17 months from the day that book was released for the ox to grow up. Only then did it begin carrying a full-time salary for me. That 17 month period was one of the most difficult times I've ever faced as I attempted to balance working two full-time jobs – one that paid the bills and the other, my dream job, that I hoped would someday pay the bills. It was the hardest I have ever worked and also one of the most rewarding times of my life as I witnessed the birth of an ox and watched it grow up to produce an **abundant harvest**.

Throughout the process, I have maintained financial margin for our business. I have never allowed the business to spend all of its money. The mission of our work is too important to jeopardize it with an empty bank account.

Rate Yourself
"Establish Substantial Financial Margin for Your Oxen"

1	2	3	4	5	6	7	8	9	10

7. If Married, Be in Agreement With Your Spouse About the Ox.

Oxen require management and can consume enormous amounts of time, energy, and money. As a result, it is important to be in agreement with your spouse regarding the reasons for owning oxen. While the level of involvement of your spouse might be vastly different in the management of the ox, oxen ownership will impact a marriage relationship.

If you are married, here are some great questions to ask each other when pondering the birthing or acquisition of an ox.

- Why do we want this ox?
- Is it worth the time we are going to invest?
- Is it worth the cost we must pay?
- Is it worth the energy we will expend?
- What impact will this ox have on our relationship?
- Should we work together on this ox?
- What impact will this ox have on our children?
- What impact will this ox have on our extended family?

The importance of unity cannot be overstated. Many times one spouse is always willing to risk everything while the other values stability and despises any risk. Serious conversations will ensue. The discussion might even grow tense and stressful.

During conversations with my bride, I discovered there is nothing more important to her than maintaining substantial financial margin – both for our personal household and within each of our businesses. She does not enjoy taking risks and values stability. If I choose to spend all of our money, both personally and for our businesses, I will negatively impact our relationship.

At times there will be genuine disagreements over whether or not to pursue an ox. Because of the significant impact that oxen can have on the marriage relationship, I highly recommend pausing the decision until all issues are addressed. It is just not worth it. No amount of abundant harvest will ever fix a broken marriage relationship.

Rate Yourself
"If Married, Be in Agreement With Your Spouse About the Ox"

1	2	3	4	5	6	7	8	9	10

8. *Be Generous*

We are challenged throughout Scripture to live generously. I Timothy 6:18 shares that we are *"to do good, to be rich in good deeds, and to be generous and willing to share."* A key benefit of having an **abundant harvest** is the ability to live generous lives! There really is nothing better. By establishing generosity as a core value of whatever ox you may acquire or birth, you are able to maximize the impact of your life.

Make it a point to live a life of generosity. Bless those who are in great need. Fund causes that you deeply believe in. There is a refining process that happens within a person as they intentionally focus on giving. When you see the needs of others, it changes your perspective of the world. It helps you understand that any abundant harvest you may achieve must be used to help others.

Are you living a life of generosity? Let me press in on this. Using the table provided, write the names of the individuals and organizations to whom you have given financial gifts within the past 12 months.

Person or Organization	Amount

As you look over your list, are you satisfied with your giving? Even more importantly, would an outside auditor review your giving and convict you of being generous? I want to be found guilty of living a generous life!

If you are living a generous life without an abundant harvest, you will have no problem living generously when you win with money!

Rate Yourself
"Be Generous"

1	2	3	4	5	6	7	8	9	10

If you apply these eight principles, you will be well on your way to successful oxen ownership. Hopefully, you have found that you are on track, but perhaps you have identified some areas that need work. I encourage you to summarize your ratings in the table provided on the next page, and then establish a few next steps you can take to move toward your goals.

Action Plan: Preparing To Own Oxen										
"Develop a Plan for Your Life"	1	2	3	4	5	6	7	8	9	10
Steps I need to take										
"Prepare and Live by a Budget"	1	2	3	4	5	6	7	8	9	10
Steps I need to take										
"Seek God's Wisdom"	1	2	3	4	5	6	7	8	9	10
Steps I need to take										
"Seek Godly Wisdom"	1	2	3	4	5	6	7	8	9	10
Steps I need to take										
"Establish Substantial Financial Margin for Your Household"	1	2	3	4	5	6	7	8	9	10
Steps I need to take										
"Establish Substantial Financial Margin for Your Oxen"	1	2	3	4	5	6	7	8	9	10
Steps I need to take										
"If Married, Be in Agreement With Your Spouse About the Ox"	1	2	3	4	5	6	7	8	9	10
Steps I need to take										
"Be Generous"	1	2	3	4	5	6	7	8	9	10
Steps I need to take										

7

Oxen in Action

In this chapter, we will examine several real-world examples of oxen. These examples are provided to help you become fully aware that this principle working all around us. It is my hope that these examples will help you gain another level of knowledge, and inspire and further equip you to reap an abundant harvest!

1. *Company Stock Investment*

Many companies are publicly owned. This means virtually anyone with available money can purchase a piece of ownership of the company. For example, Honeywell, the huge multinational manufacturing company that makes everything from airplane engines to consumer products, has more than 780.57 million outstanding shares of stock.[iv] As long as a person has enough money to purchase stock, ownership can happen instantaneously with the purchase of at least one share. While this small purchase will not gain you direct access to the CEO, you will gain other ownership privileges including the right to participate in sharing company profits as well as any increase in company value.

Think about the power of this ox for a minute. By choosing to save enough money to acquire shares of stock, your money now has acquired the potential for future earnings. Through the simple purchase of just one share of company stock, you have tied into the collective power of all the company's products, services, brand power, and employee skills, abilities, and energy. Simply amazing! Even more amazing is the fact that this type of ox may require little to zero tending after it is purchased!

Of course, stock purchases also carry the risk of loss. If one were to own only one ox, what would happen if that ox died suddenly? The owner would experience a tragic loss of both the ox and the potential for an abundant harvest! As a result, I personally choose to never have more than ten percent of my money invested into a single company stock, so if one of my oxen died, my entire future financial livelihood is not at stake.

2. *Mutual Fund & ETF Investment*

Mutual Funds and Exchange-Traded Funds (ETFs) have become extremely popular ways to diversify investments. If all money were placed into a single company stock, the potential exists for the ox to die and leave the investor with nothing. To mitigate this risk of this "all the eggs in one basket" scenario, mutual funds allow an investor to purchase a portion of many company stocks or bonds with a single share purchase. The investor's money is pooled together with money provided by hundreds of thousands of additional investors. The mutual fund company uses this combined money to purchase stocks and bonds of thousands of companies.

It would be financially impossible for most investors to purchase individual stock in hundreds of companies, but mutual fund and ETF providers make it possible by creating their own "share" of ownership. By purchasing a single share of the mutual fund or ETF, the investor actually becomes the proud owner of tiny fractions of all the companies owned by the fund. In other words, the purchase of a share of the fund allows the investor to become partial owner of a vast field of oxen that are corralled together and moving in the same direction.

Mutual Fund
Company #1 - $1,000,000
Company #2 - $1,000,000
Company #3 - $1,000,000
Company #4 - $1,000,000
Company #5 - $1,000,000
Company #6 - $1,000,000
Company #7 - $1,000,000
Company #8 - $1,000,000
Company #9 - $1,000,000
Company #10 - $1,000,000
Company #11 - $1,000,000
Company #12 - $1,000,000
Company #13 - $1,000,000
Company #14 - $1,000,000
Company #15 - $1,000,000
Company #16 - $1,000,000

Figure 1 *Example Mutual Fund*

Look at the mutual fund example in Figure 1. In this mutual fund, the managers of the fund have purchased $1,000,000 of stock in 16 different companies – an impossible feat for most people. This is where mutual fund (and similar type fund) companies provide tremendous value. They allow individual investors to purchase a "share" of the mutual fund itself at a more manageable price. For instance, Figure 2 shows that a share of the fund can be purchased for ten dollars. For just ten dollars, the investor is able to own a fractional piece of ownership in 16 different companies. Through this type of stock purchase, investors are able to diversify their investments at a price they can afford and avoid placing all of their eggs into one basket.

Mutual Fund	
	Company #1 - $1,000,000
	Company #2 - $1,000,000
	Company #3 - $1,000,000
	Company #4 - $1,000,000
1 share of the fund = $10	Company #5 - $1,000,000
	Company #6 - $1,000,000
	Company #7 - $1,000,000
	Company #8 - $1,000,000
	Company #9 - $1,000,000
	Company #10 - $1,000,000
	Company #11 - $1,000,000
	Company #12 - $1,000,000
	Company #13 - $1,000,000
	Company #14 - $1,000,000
	Company #15 - $1,000,000
	Company #16 - $1,000,000

Figure 2 *Example Mutual Fund – Individual Share Outlined*

It is highly unlikely that all the companies would fail at the same time so this reduces risk and makes mutual funds and ETFs attractive for the average stock and bond investor.

3. *Commercial Rental Real Estate*

Commercial rental real estate can become a huge ox that can carry a huge load. Consider the owner of a retail shopping center with 19 retail spaces available for rent. The owner incurs tremendous costs to birth this ox. Incredible amounts of money are spent to:

- Conduct feasibility studies
- Research, identify, negotiate, and acquire land
- Obtain appropriate zoning and restrictions
- Seek legal counsel
- Complete engineering and architectural drawings
- Build the facility
- Advertise and market

These costs do not include the ongoing expense of insuring and maintaining the facilities, but even with up-front knowledge of these costs, the investor feels it is a wise decision to birth the ox. Before the building phase begins, five of the units are leased with businesses who want to be at this location. As the building phase is completed, another five units are leased. Within a year, all 19 store fronts are leased. This type of ox will pull a huge load! In fact, this is not just one ox. The 19 businesses leasing space are individual oxen who help pull the load.

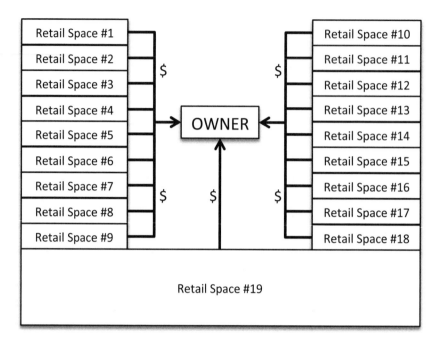

Think about how the success of the commercial rental real estate owner is dependent upon each investor who has placed their business in one of the retail spaces. Essentially, the owner has put a yoke on each of the companies leasing space. As the individual companies succeed, so will the owner. In other words, success is dependent upon not only the owner, but also the individual companies leasing space. If the owner becomes greedy and increases the rental rate to a point that individual companies can no longer pay, they will collapse. As individual oxen leave because of the increased burden, those who remain will be forced to carry the additional load left behind. This could cause the entire retail shopping center to fail!

Another common example of a commercial rental real estate oxen is "owner occupied" property. Consider an eye doctor who needs an office. She builds a great practice in a great location. Because she recognizes the value of oxen, she builds a facility that can accommodate two other businesses: a small café and an insurance agency. Because of its location, the facility provides excellent value to the owners of these two other companies. Since they are not prepared for the ownership of a building, renting suits their businesses perfectly. The great news is that the eye doctor does not have to bear the cost of owning and operating her facility because the rent paid by the two companies more than covers the monthly ownership costs of the entire facility! This allows her practice to operate at higher margins while at the same time gaining an increase in net worth as the building increases in value.

Are you beginning to see the power of owning oxen?

4. *Residential Rental Real Estate*

Residential rental real estate is one of the most common examples of oxen ownership that people choose to acquire or birth. Consider a builder who clearly understands the housing market where he owns and operates his construction business. As well-priced houses become available, he purchases them with the intention of fixing them up and leasing them. Even thought this type of acquisition requires substantial financial margin, it is possible for most people to accomplish this within five years of beginning their oxen acquisition journey.

Even though it takes a loan from the bank to pay for the home, the builder sees tremendous potential. By maintaining substantial cash margin, he is able to avoid repercussions of negative financial events such as renter non-payment, surprise maintenance and repair costs, and vacancies. The first house is rented right away, and the monthly rent payments more than cover the cost of the mortgage as well as property taxes and ongoing repair costs. Within a few years, the builder is able to acquire, improve, and lease two more houses.

Fast forward twenty years. The houses are now completely paid off, and rental income is still arriving every single month. The oxen are producing an abundant harvest!

Consider the following question for a moment. Who paid for the houses? The renters or the owner? The renters paid for the houses! The owner merely took the rent payments and sent them to the bank. Then one day, the houses are completely paid for with all future rental income coming to whom – the renters or the owner? The **owner**!

This type of ox produces an abundant harvest in two different ways:

1. Monthly rent
2. Home value increase

While the immediately apparent harvest is the monthly rental income, the increase in home value is less instantaneous. The houses actually tripled in value over the twenty year period. These oxen have already pulled a tremendous load and continue to deliver an abundant harvest!

5. *Land Real Estate*

"Land. They are not making any more of it." I have heard this phrase spoken many times, and with the exception of a few volcanoes producing new islands out in the ocean, it's true! As a result, land values have historically increased over time. This is perhaps the most basic form of oxen as it has been in existence since the beginning of time. People have used land to achieve an abundant harvest with various crops, animals, trees and plants. It has been used for recreation as well as construction. Tremendous wealth has also been achieved in, on, and under land by discovering and harvesting key minerals, metals, gas, and oil.

6. *Restaurants*

Many individuals have done quite well in the restaurant business. From roadside hot dog stands to fine dining restaurants, opportunity abounds for this type of ox to deliver profits. Regardless of the type of establishment, there are several common factors to success: location, great food, tremendous service, and value.

I know a couple who had a dream of creating a high-end, white tablecloth restaurant that would bring incredible foods from around the world to their city. They worked very hard to make their dream come true. This included obtaining certifications from a renowned culinary institute, creating wonderful meals and desserts, and locating "the perfect place" for the restaurant. They invested extreme amounts of their personal money, time, and effort into their dream, and it has paid off handsomely as the restaurant has yielded an abundant harvest. In the process, their hard work garnered something they could only dream of – worldwide attention.

This type of ox has two types of value:

1.   The ongoing profits generated by operating the business
2.   Actual value of the business (should they choose to sell one day)

7.   *Franchises*

Franchise opportunities exist in many types of businesses. While starting a restaurant on your own can sound very exciting, it can also be exhausting and trying. Those who enjoy the restaurant business but want to follow a proven model for success can do so by purchasing franchise rights. McDonald's, Papa John's, Quizno's, and Subway are just a few examples of franchise restaurants.

In this approach, the parent company is a huge ox that carries a part of the load for the individual franchisee. The franchisee must pay a portion of their revenue to the parent company, and in return, the parent company provides ongoing marketing and promotional initiatives, market research, quality standards implementation and control, and new product development.

8.   *Any Small Business*

Any type of small business has the potential to be an ox that could grow into a herd of oxen.

You might enjoy cutting and styling hair. With some focused effort, you can obtain the necessary certifications and start your business. The business might begin in your house or by paying booth rent at a salon. Profits from this business can be used to purchase the salon and all of its booths. This allows you to capture the power of all the oxen working there.

Lawn care might be your specialty. Load up the lawn mower and knock on every door in the subdivision asking your neighbors for yard work they would pay you to complete. You can establish long-term contracts with dozens of families and businesses and hire employees to fulfill the work.

Maybe trucking is something you love to do. You can obtain a job driving for a freight company. By keeping your personal costs low, you can save a lot of money that can be used to purchase a truck of your own. As that truck helps you produce a profit, you can purchase a second truck. You might end up a forty truck operation yielding an incredibly abundant harvest!

Maybe you love visiting gas station convenience stores. Why not own one? While saving money to purchase one, learn how to operate a convenience store successfully. This will allow you to prove to yourself and others in your sphere of influence that you are trustworthy with money and completely understand the convenience store business. By using your saved money and money invested by others who believe in your dream, you can purchase a struggling store. As that store is restored to health and begins producing a profit, you can use the profits to purchase another one. You could end up owning fifty stores. Fifty convenience stores can produce an amazingly abundant harvest!

I had a dream of equipping people to accomplish far more than they ever thought possible with their finances. My dream began to become reality when I chose to invest money into it. I eliminated all of my non-house debt so I could give up over half of my income to position myself to serve others. I began spending time and energy to write a blog now known as the wildly popular JosephSangl.com. As a result, a few speaking opportunities became available. Then more requests came in. Then even more. I spent thousands of dollars to self-publish my first book, *I Was Broke. Now I'm Not.*, because no publisher was interested.

I'll never forget the day that two thousand books were delivered to my house. My bride was so thrilled as I lined them up in the middle of our living room. "Do we really have to store these here?" she asked. "Absolutely." I replied, "As we watch every box leave, it will be a testimony to God's grace as He funds this dream." Imagine our excitement and gratitude as we watched every single box leave that living room in a very short period of time!

What began as a dream has grown into a world-wide organization serving churches and businesses around the globe. The ox has grown up, birthed numerous additional oxen, and truly yielded an abundant harvest. It is the reason I have written this book. I know that if I could do it, so can you!

8

Identify Potential Oxen

This chapter will share strategies for identifying oxen you could potentially birth or acquire. As you consider this information, please remember that this process requires time and energy – sometimes a lot of it, but also remember that the potential of achieving an abundant harvest is worth the effort!

1. *Identify Your Passion*

Passion ignites a fire in people like nothing else does. I have seen passion transform extremely shy and quiet people into incredibly dynamic public speakers. Nearly every great organization is built on the passion of its leaders. John Wesley, the great minister from the 18th century famously said, "Catch on fire with enthusiasm and people will come for miles to watch you burn."v Passionate people have the ability to ignite contagious enthusiasm that can seem unquenchable.

Passionate people will do what others will not ordinarily do, and this provides the avenue for them to accomplish the extraordinary! They refuse to give in even when conventional wisdom says it is time to stop. Ask any person who has birthed an ox this question: "Have you had moments where you thought your dream was not going to make it?" Nearly every one will tell you their story of surviving significant challenges while in pursuit of their dream. Follow their response with this question: "What kept you going during that difficult time?" Almost every time, the core of their passion will be revealed in their answer.

Passion will provide energy even when you are exhausted. It will keep you focused on what is most important. When you clearly understand your passion, it will help you answer difficult questions before they are even asked.

Here are some good questions to ask yourself when identifying your passion:

1. What fires you up?
2. What is your dream job?
3. If money were no object, what would you do?

Famous time study expert, Frank Bunker Gilbreth, Sr. (of *Cheaper By The Dozen* fame), disappointed his mother when he informed her he was going to be a bricklayer. Recovering from the fact that her dreams for her son had just been dashed, Frank's mother challenged him to become the best bricklayer in the world. He did just that. Through his bricklaying job, Frank discovered his real passion – efficiency. After a short time on the job, Frank was pointing out multiple ways his boss could become more efficient at laying brick. Despite continued objections and outbursts from his boss, Frank continued to point out additional ways to improve the process. This frustrated his boss so much that he shouted, "I'm warning you; stop bothering me or this brick goes in your mouth - edgewise!" vi

Of course, Frank could not stop talking about becoming more efficient because it was his passion. Passion made Frank keep talking; he just couldn't help himself. He went on to become the "Father of Time-Studies" and transformed industry and the military with his passionate pursuit of efficiency.

Identify your passion, and you might just discover an ox or two. Who knows? Your passion might even help you change the world!

2. *Identify Your Skills and Abilities*

What are you good at? A very revealing way to determine this is to ask the following question to those who know you best: "What do you think I'm really good at?" Balance the responses with what you already know about yourself. People who love us sometimes shield brutal truth. We have all heard the person sing terribly, but they believe they are terrific because their parents lied to them and told them they could sing amazingly well.

I have discovered two truths about any true gifting and ability:

    A. People notice it and remark about it to the individual
    B. People notice it and make remarks about it to others

Birthing or acquiring oxen is difficult enough on its own, but attempting to lead oxen far from your gifting and ability can be completely demoralizing – regardless of how much of an abundant harvest it helps you produce. This is why so many family businesses fail (oxen death) under the direction of the second generation. The business was started because of the passion of its founder, and it maximized the gifting of that leader. The second generation leader may have no passion or gifting for that business, but attempts to lead it out of obligation or because it is producing an abundant harvest.

You will maximize your life when you match your passion with your talents. It can lead to unstoppable oxen allowing you to serve multitudes of people while also funding your biggest dreams!

3. *Identify Your Dream*

Without a clear dream, it is easy to waste years of life and a lot of money and still end up with no oxen. If you could choose your ultimate dream ox or herd of oxen, what would it look like? Who would work with you? What customers would you serve? What product(s) and/or service(s) would you deliver? Where in the world would you conduct business? How much money would it take? How many people would be needed? What type of harvest would it produce? What would you do with that harvest?

Every great thing that is accomplished starts with a dream. The noted leadership guru, Dr. John C. Maxwell, has written a tremendous book, *Put Your Dream To The Test,* that helps people fully flesh out their dreams and answer the question, "Is my dream *really* my dream?" I highly recommend Dr. Maxwell's book, especially when considering "making the leap" into pursuing a dream with all of your energy.

4. *Clearly Define How Your Ox Will Serve and Help People*

When you know just how your ox will allow you to serve and help people, it will further fuel your passion to accomplish the dream. How will your dream serve and help people? In order for any ox to produce an abundant harvest, people must find enough value in the provided product or service that they are willing to pay for it. This means that understanding how your oxen will serve people is essential.

General Electric has made light bulbs for decades. Their light bulbs help me see more clearly in my office, house, and while driving my car at night. This business has been a tremendously long-lasting ox for GE because they have identified people's real needs for lighting and have delivered valuable solutions people are willing to pay for. In fact, their light bulb ox has delivered such a harvest, it has allowed GE to use the abundance to start, expand, and purchase many businesses making it one of the largest companies in the world. It all started with one man's dream of utilizing electricity to provide lighting to the world. You may have heard of the man who dreamed this dream and knew exactly how well it would serve people. It is Thomas Edison.[vii]

5. *Determine How Your Ox Can Earn a Profit*

It is wonderful to have an ox. It is even better when the ox allows you to utilize your best abilities and talents, but this is just the start. A bigger question must be asked:

How will this ox earn a profit?

In order to experience an abundant harvest, there must be profit. I am always amused at people who proudly say their organization is non-profit as if it is superior to operating a for-profit company. The truth is ALL organizations must achieve a profit. Even non-profits must earn a profit, or they will run out of money and cease to exist. Nearly every non-profit experiences funding challenges, and if the organization has chosen to spend everything without prioritizing financial margin, they could run out of money. This can cause enormous harm to their mission, even to the point of failure.

For any dream to become an ox that produces an abundant harvest, it must earn a profit. Do you know how your dream will produce revenue and earn money?

Maybe your dream is to write a children's book complete with beautiful color illustrations and hardcover. There's just one problem. No publisher is interested in your book. You have tested your dream and have had others comment very enthusiastically about the book. You determined that you must pursue the dream further because it will allow you to serve children and their parents with an entertaining and enjoyable reading experience. You can just imagine the smiles on the faces of those children as their parents read them this book – a book you birthed!

Since delaying your dream is not an option, your passion propels you to self-publish the book. This means you must invest both the time and money to work with a printer to produce a thousand books. Once the investment is made, this dream can earn a profit by selling enough books to cover the costs of writing, illustrating, copyrighting, typesetting, editing, marketing, and selling the book. Do you see how it works? Passion, energy, time, and a willingness to do what others will not do will enable the dream to become an ox that possesses the ability to produce an abundant harvest.

Here is another example. Suppose there is a young man who dreams of selling insurance. While many people are less than inspired to deal with insurance because of its cost and the confusing variety of insurance products available, Paul dreams of helping consumers choose the right products for their families. It is an approach he calls "Insurance Made Simple." To obtain the right to sell insurance products, he must spend time and money to study and pass the necessary certification examinations. He also must cover all his business expenses which include travel, Internet, computer, web site, and lead-generation. He has clearly identified how this dream will earn a profit through commissions earned on each product sold. A profit will be achieved by earning more commissions than the money spent to achieve those sales.

Consider Paul's dream a little further. Suppose he wants to serve far more people with his "Insurance Made Simple" approach than he could accomplish on his own. To do this, he must hire additional employees. A profit will be earned when those employees produce more sales than it costs to pay their salaries and benefits as well as the additional office and business expenses that will be incurred by having additional employees. This expanded dream could yield an extraordinarily abundant harvest!

An example of Paul's financial plan of how his dream will earn a profit is outlined on the next page. As you can see, he is expecting to produce a profit of $178,000. While it is impossible to perfectly predict sales and costs, this process of planning is what will ensure that an abundant harvest is achieved.

Products Sold	Expected Sales Commissions	Expenses	Expected Costs
Life Insurance	$100,000	Travel	$10,000
Auto Insurance	$250,000	Internet	$2,000
Health Insurance	$250,000	Computer	$10,000
		Web Site	$15,000
		Office (including utilities)	$30,000
		Employees	$250,000
		Employee Benefits	$50,000
		Licenses & Fees	$5,000
		Paid Lead Generation	$50,000
TOTAL SALES REVENUE	$600,000	**TOTAL EXPENSES**	$422,000
NET PROFIT		**$178,000**	

Use the form provided to demonstrate how your dream will produce a profit. Remember that it is okay to use estimations as it is impossible to predict the future to the exact penny. Don't be overly concerned if you can't immediately determine how your dream will produce a profit. If you experience difficulties demonstrating how your dream will pay off, set the plan aside for a few days or weeks and then revisit it. You will have a heightened awareness of the need for your dream to yield a profit. Use this time to pray and seek wisdom. Watch other businesses to see how they are generating profits. As you have conversations with those you trust and observe other businesses in action, you might just discover a way your ox could generate a profit.

Products & Services Sold	Expected Annual Sales Commissions	Expenses	Expected Annual Costs
TOTAL SALES REVENUE		**TOTAL EXPENSES**	
NET PROFIT			

6. *Identify the True Cost of the Ox*

While it is always important to understand the financial implications of birthing or acquiring an ox, it is even more important to consider its overall total costs. There *is* such a thing as an ox that costs too much!

Consider the relational costs. Even if an ox produces an incredibly abundant financial harvest, it isn't worth it if the costs include a divorce and estranged relationships with your children and family!

Think about the time costs. How much of your time will this dream take? Remember, the goal of oxen acquisition is for the oxen to carry a load you cannot carry on your own and to produce a harvest even when you are sleeping! Always remember that work is infinite. Choose to do work that makes the most impact.

Ponder the stress, pressure, and emotional costs. How much can you take without severely affecting your health? Are you able to deal with crazy financial stress? For example, if you cannot deal well with rapidly changing environments and you are considering starting a stock trading business, you should immediately reconsider your dream!

One cost regularly overlooked is the cost of birthing or pursuing additional oxen. By choosing to pursue an ox, you may have to delay or completely cease the pursuit of other oxen. In economics, this cost is described as the "opportunity cost" – the next best alternative use of your money, time, and effort. A great question to always ask is, "If I choose to not pursue this ox, what alternative ox or oxen would be the next best use of my time, energy, and money?" This is a great exercise that helps you determine if the ox you are currently pursuing really is the best for you.

Use the following table to list the ox or oxen you want to acquire and then ponder alternative oxen you could use your time, energy, and money pursuing.

Preferred Ox(en)	Alternative Ox(en) I Could Pursue

This exercise has been valuable to me in two key ways:

    a. **Confirmation** This process helps me clearly confirm whether or not the oxen I am considering are the best use of my time, energy, and money.

    b. **Identification of New Opportunities** As I list other oxen I could pursue and truly allow myself to consider the alternatives, I am identifying oxen I could potentially pursue in the future!

It is impossible to identify all of the true time, energy, and financial costs of potential oxen, but by diligently using this process, you will certainly limit surprises.

7. *Conduct a Strengths, Weaknesses, Opportunities, and Threats Analysis (SWOT Analysis)*

At this point of the oxen identification process, you should conduct a Strengths, Weaknesses, Opportunities, and Threats Analysis (SWOT Analysis). This is a tool that has worked extremely well at every organization I have served.

Strengths

What makes you confident in your dream? Write down all the items that you view as strengths in the plan you have developed. These can include individual characteristics such as your passion and education as well as strategic and intellectual strengths like patent protections or a special top secret recipe. It can also include the people who have agreed to help you as well as your financial situation.

Weaknesses

Every plan usually has at least a few key weaknesses. What part of your plan makes your knees tremble? This does not mean you should not pursue the ox, but it is important to identify these points because it opens your eyes to potential risks and allows you to make appropriate adjustments.

Since it is easy to see the world through rose-colored glasses when you are fired up about an idea, consider obtaining help in identifying specific weaknesses and risks. This help can come in the form of seeking God's wisdom and through the counsel of your mentors.

Opportunities

What new opportunities could this new ox provide? Would it open doors for you to reach the next level? Perhaps it will allow you to fulfill a life-long dream. Maybe it could help you expand the reach of your other oxen.

When I acquired INJOY Stewardship Solutions, a premier provider of capital stewardship campaign consulting services, it provided an avenue for the I Was Broke. Now I'm Not. (IWBNIN) team to introduce its products and resources to thousands of leaders who did not know the IWBNIN organization even existed. This was an incredible opportunity for one ox to help another one thrive!

I find it amusing and incredibly smart that Unilever, the giant multi-national consumer goods conglomerate, owns Slim-Fast dieting food products and two ice cream brands: Good Humor and Ben & Jerry's.[viii] They have identified a way to serve people's sweet tooth and also their need to slim down after eating so many calories!

Threats

What would make your plan fail? Are there similar oxen owned by a competitor that could jeopardize your business? Would acquiring these oxen burden your finances to the point that you could collapse financially? If you are considering purchasing an existing ox, there might be legal or environment issues that must be addressed.

Most people who are embarking on a journey to birth or acquire an ox can easily identify their threats by answering the question, "Why do I fear making this decision?" I have discovered that writing threats down on paper can make them seem manageable and less intimidating.

Now it is time for you complete a SWOT Analysis for the ox you are considering birthing or acquiring. Use the table provided to do this.

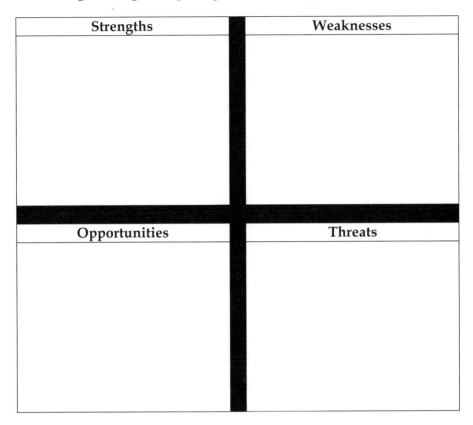

Strengths	Weaknesses

Opportunities	Threats

This process makes you ask critical questions *before* spending time, energy, and money. It has saved so much heartache for many people. I strongly encourage you to always take the time to complete this activity each time you are considering pursuing a new ox.

8. *Seek Wisdom*

In the same way that you seek wisdom as you are preparing for oxen ownership, be sure to continue this practice as you identify the oxen you will actually acquire. While you have already identified potential mentors in Chapter 6, it is important to further evaluate your mentors as you take the actual steps to purchase or birth your own oxen. I have found it helpful to seek counsel from two types of people.

Wisdom Type 1 – *People who have "Been there. Done that."*

It is always humbling and quite an honor to gain wisdom from people who have the battle scars of owning oxen. It takes courage to ask others for help. Pride always makes me want to "be the man" and do everything on my own, but pride was what kept me broke! Drop the pride and muster up the courage to seek counsel from people who have "Been there. Done that."

Find someone who has successfully owned oxen for a decade or longer and ask them questions about how they succeeded. Here are some great questions to ask someone of this caliber:

- Did you ever experience fear as you launched out to own oxen?
- What is the biggest lesson you learned that you wished you knew before you started?
- What are the top three things that have allowed you to remain successful for so long?
- Did you have any failures or struggles along the way?
- What has been your favorite part of owning oxen?
- Who have you learned from?
- Who do you know that I should know?
- Would you mentor me as I launch my own endeavor?

Most people who have experienced success would love nothing more than to share their story. After all, their oxen have carried a huge load for them, a load that they could have never borne on their own. Leaders who have experienced an abundant harvest are among the most generous people on the face of the earth, and most feel honored to help others with their journey.

Take a moment to write down the names of a few experienced leaders from whom you could learn.

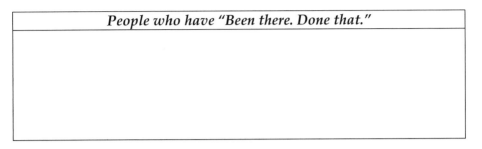

People who have "Been there. Done that."

Now take a moment to think about how you will ask them to mentor you. Lunch appointments have always worked well for me – especially when I offer to buy! Set up a meeting at their office or at Starbucks. Do not waste their time. Bring a list of questions, a notebook, and an open mind to each meeting, and be prepared to learn.

Wisdom Type 2 – *People who love you and have no vested financial interest in your potential oxen*

People who have known you a long time have an ability to speak truth in a way that no one else can. My family has been very blessed, and my brothers have achieved some tremendous accomplishments. However, when we get together, we don't call each other Doctor, Pastor, Reverend, Director or Chief. Those titles are all dropped the minute we we walk in the door. We call each other by our first names or the nicknames (both the good and bad ones) we picked up as we grew up together. Truth is spoken plainly, and there is no embellishment. Those who love me have given me invaluable feedback along the way.

Remember the key words that describe this category of people. These are people who truly *love* you. It is their whole-hearted desire to see you win. They celebrate all your victories without envy. This is important because many people mistakenly ask a dysfunctional family member to give them feedback on a dream. This can be a dream-robbing experience.

After sharing your dream with those who love you, ask them for feedback. Below are some great conversation starters.

- What do you think of my dream?
- Did any alarm bells go off in your head as you heard me share my dream?
- Do you think it will work?
- Am I crazy to think I can actually do this?
- You know me so well. What are some important areas that I have a tendency to be overly optimistic about?
- Can you see me doing this?
- Will you pray for me?
- Would you be okay with me bouncing ideas off of you every now and then?

As I began my journey to acquire oxen, the conversations I had with those who love me were incredibly meaningful – both for me and them! I made better decisions because of their input, and they have joy knowing that they helped me successfully launch my dream.

Take a moment to write down a list of people who *love* you and with whom you want to share your dream.

People who love you and have no vested financial interest in your potential oxen

In some cases, you might discover that some people fit into both categories. This is a wonderful situation to find yourself in as you have people with experience and wisdom who love you and have your best at heart, ensuring that your conversations with them are even richer.

In II Chronicles 1:7, God said to Solomon, *"Ask for whatever you want me to give you."* Solomon could have asked for so many things, but because he requested *wisdom*, God gave him wealth, riches, and honor. I have discovered this is usually the truth – those who seek out wisdom achieve financial success and a measure of honor.

Those are eight steps you can take to identify oxen that will have the highest potential for success for you.

1. *Identify Your Passion*
2. *Identify Your Skills and Abilities*
3. *Identify Your Dream*
4. *Clearly Define How Your Ox Will Serve and Help People*
5. *Determine How Your Ox Can Earn a Profit*
6. *Identify the True Cost of the Ox*
7. *Conduct a Strengths, Weaknesses, Opportunities, and Threats Analysis (SWOT Analysis)*
8. *Seek Wisdom*

If you have never owned oxen, it might seem to be an extremely lengthy and intimidating process. It can seem like you are attempting to eat an entire elephant all at once, but I know you can do this! Follow these steps, consume the elephant one bite at a time, and soon you will have an ox or two working hard on your behalf and be on your way to an abundant harvest!

9

Acquire Oxen

The time for talking is over. You understand the power of oxen and have done everything possible to prepare for the birth or acquisition of your ox. Your eyes have become opened to the oxen that other people have working for them. You have taken the time to seek wisdom. All the necessary financial decisions have been made and put into place. It is now time to get an ox!

There are several ways to acquire or birth an ox.

1. Use Your Skill, Ability, and Time and Another Person's Money

If you have a great skill or ability and possess the time necessary to acquire or birth an ox, it is quite possible for you to raise the funds from other people to fund your dream. In the mid-1970's a young man named Bill Gates was attending Harvard. He possessed an amazing ability to write computer code. It took just one meeting with a major computer company for the leaders of that company to recognize Bill's great ability. They chose to fund Bill's work, and the rest is history. Microsoft has become the world's preeminent provider of software.[ix]

Perhaps you also possess amazing talent but lack sufficient funds to finance your dream. While this presents a substantial challenge, your goal should be to seek an audience with others who will recognize your ability and help fund your next steps.

This is the true for many people who have the gift of singing. A person may be able to sing incredibly well, but it can take the financial horsepower of a studio to record and distribute the ox. In this case, the ox is an album. A person with the gift of acting may need to leverage the financial strength of a production company in order to help them birth their ox – a movie.

If it is your desire to remain debt free while birthing an ox, this can be accomplished. Instead of structuring a repayment schedule with the individuals or entity who provided the financial resources, offer them a share of the financial results or an ownership stake.

This type of ox requires active management, and you only possess a limited amount of time and energy. It is for this reason that most people are usually able to own just a few of this type of oxen. The individual who invested only money into your dream will spend very little of their time and energy on this ox because you are doing the work for them. This means you have essentially become an ox for them! It is a win-win situation for both of you because it is through their financial investment you are able to accomplish the dream.

2. *Use Your Money and Another Person's Skill, Ability, and Time.*

This is commonly referred to as "having your money working for you." In this case, you become the "financial investor" and enable someone else to leverage their skills, abilities, and time toward birthing or acquiring an ox. This type of ox requires less active management, so you are able to manage more oxen like this versus the type that require your individual skill, ability, and time.

A stock investment is a perfect example. When you purchase stock ownership in a company, it allows you to benefit from the collective efforts of everyone employed there. Every single day the employees show up to work to help their company produce a profit, and you are entitled to your share of it – even if you slept or vacationed while they worked!

As you gather money for oxen acquisition, look for individuals who possess tremendous talent and have a great idea, but who need some financial assistance to bring the dream to life. By investing financially in their dream, you are enabling their talent and passion to achieve an abundant harvest for all involved. This type of investment carries significant risk, but it can be minimized by writing clear contracts and asking pertinent questions before investing to clearly define when, where, and how the money will be utilized.

3. *Use a Combination of #1 and #2*

The truth is that most oxen will require a combination of your money, skill, ability, and time, and it is rare that one can acquire an ox without the personal investment of these things. Oxen ownership comes at a substantial price, and it will take your money and effort to experience the abundant harvest that oxen bring.

4. *Finance Your Acquisition*

Finance it? It is true. I, Joseph Sangl, have written these very words. And yes, I am the very same Joseph Sangl who routinely writes about the importance of pursuing debt freedom and the liberty of owing no one. For those who know me best, you may believe I have lost my mind.

I can confirm that I have not lost my mind. While I believe everyone should pursue debt freedom and enjoy the liberty of owing nothing to anyone, I clearly understand the substantial cost of acquiring oxen. It might not be possible for many to pay cash for their ox. I would never have been able to acquire my education oxen (two degrees – bachelor of science in mechanical engineering from Purdue University and a master of business administration from Clemson University) without student loans. I could not have bought my real estate ox (my home) without a mortgage loan.

While it should always be the goal to birth or acquire a business with a 100 percent cash purchase, a loan could be necessary to complete the deal. Whenever you are considering financing your oxen acquisition or birth, be sure to ask yourself the following questions:

- Is there any possible way I can pay cash for this ox?
- If I refuse to obtain debt, is there still a way I can acquire or birth this ox?

- Will this ox go up or down in value while I am paying off the loan?
- With what degree of certainty can I expect this ox to yield a profit and repay the borrowed money?
- Will the ox be able to repay the borrowed amount within five years or less?
- If the ox dies unexpectedly, could I still repay the borrowed amount from other sources?

Here are four ways to fund the birth or acquisition of your ox:

a. Bank Finance

This is the most common form of financing, and most people have obtained money this way at least once in their life through either the financing of a car, home, or the use of a credit card. In this arrangement, a loan request is made by the potential borrower (oxen acquirer) to their lending institution. Based upon the belief of the bank's loan officers in the ox's ability to repay the money, a decision is made to loan the money or to deny the request.

The benefit of working with a bank is that they usually have clear lending processes and can challenge you to ask very important questions you may not have. If acquiring an ox, it also allows the current owner to receive all of their money up-front, and allows you to deal solely with the bank in the future.

b. Owner Finance

If you are acquiring an ox, you might be able to create an arrangement with the current owner in which you pay for the ox over an agreed upon period of time using profits produced by the ox. This is perhaps the oldest form of lending in the world. A very common example is when a family-run business is sold by retiring parents to their son or daughter.

Suppose a business is valued at $1,000,000. The parents could sell it to their daughter by structuring a deal where the daughter will pay her parents $100,000 per year from the business each of the next ten years. After ten years, the daughter will be the full owner of the business, and the parents will have received their $1,000,000.

Another common example is acquiring property via an owner financing arrangement. This type of financing operates in much the same way as a regular mortgage from a lending institution. A contract is written with an established borrowed amount, the specific terms for repayment including repayment period, payment frequency, and an interest rate. An amortization schedule is produced and payments commence as outlined in the agreement. Once the contract is fully satisfied, the lien is released by the original owner.

In another example, a business is being sold to one of its employees. The employee is acquiring an ox he is already highly involved in, and he firmly believes the business is a strong ox that can carry a tremendous load. Because the business does not have assets that can easily be sold, banks are unwilling to lend money. This doesn't come as a surprise to the existing owners since they have experienced lending denials throughout their ownership years. To move the deal forward, owner financing is agreed upon.

In this agreement, the past owners establish private stock for the company and agree to sell every share of stock to the buyer (and only the buyer) at a set price. The stock purchase price remains unchanged for ten years. The buyer is required to purchase a minimum amount of stock every month to ensure all the stock is purchased within the ten year period.

This deal allows the owners to sell the business in a way that provides income (without working) every month for the next ten years, and it enables the employee to acquire the ox in a way that does not overburden it. This is what is called a "win-win" situation!

Because this type of arrangement does not require a bank, the terms can be extremely flexible as long as there is agreement among all involved parties, making this a key benefit to owner financing. It is always wise to have a written agreement and to solicit the advice of a qualified attorney prior to signing it. This ensures that each part of the contract is imminently clear and neither party can conveniently "forget" something.

c. **Self Finance**

If you already have an ox or two, you might be able to finance the next ox using your own money. This is exactly how I birthed I Was Broke. Now I'm Not., LLC, a personal finance organization focused on "helping people accomplish far more than they ever thought possible." My existing oxen produced enough profit that I could establish a "birth or acquire oxen" fund.

In January 2006, I began writing my first book, *I Was Broke. Now I'm Not.* Many authors dream of the day a publisher will swoop in and pay tons of money for the right and privilege of printing and selling their book. It took just a few conversations for me to realize that I would have to find my own way to fund the publishing of my book. As writing neared completion in November 2007, I used money from my personal savings account to help birth the book. In our accounting records, I literally called it a "Loan from Joe/Jenn" because I knew that profits from the sale of this new book had to repay the money to our personal accounts in order to consider this ox successful.

I'm so glad I took the risk, as *I Was Broke. Now I'm Not.* has gone around the globe and allowed me to help tens of thousands of people – most of whom I have never even met in person.

I really do not like debt, but if I am going to owe someone, I prefer it to be me! This is the POWER of having multiple oxen. Your existing oxen can function as a bank for your future oxen!

d. Trade

Sometimes it makes sense to trade some of your current oxen for other oxen. If you have too many oxen that require active management, you can trade for oxen that require less involvement. For example, you could sell an existing restaurant that requires 20 hours of your time every week and use the money to purchase shares of a mutual fund that require zero hours of your time. You have essentially "traded" oxen with someone else. They use their money to purchase the restaurant ox which you subsequently use to purchase a new mutual fund ox.

Acquiring and birthing an ox can certainly be arduous, but it can be so very rewarding! The hard work positions you to experience an abundant harvest.

Be sure to enjoy the process. Maintain a journal that documents all the crazy things you experience as you birth and acquire your oxen. Looking back, you will be able to see how amazing the entire journey was. Your old notes will give you the confidence to move forward with the acquisition of other oxen, and provide a landmark that allows you to look forward to tremendous challenges and say, "If I was able to overcome past obstacles, I can certainly do so now!

10

Leading Oxen

Once you are an oxen owner, you might feel like you have reached the finish line, but you have really only made it to the starting line! Every ox requires leadership and guidance in order to be productive. If left alone to themselves, real oxen will not be productive. They will stand around, lay down, wander off, and eat all of the available food without working at all. It is only after you provide leadership, training, and ongoing guidance that you can capture their strength to produce an abundant harvest.

In this section, we will review several key aspects of oxen leadership and management that are essential in ensuring maximum results.

1. *Always Know the Status of Your Oxen*

This cannot be emphasized enough! It is absolutely vital to understand the status of every single ox you own. Just like real oxen, your financial oxen will go through stages of life. If you fail to monitor your herd, you could jeopardize the very existence of each ox. Proverbs 27:23 shares this exhortation: *"Be sure you know the condition of your flocks, give careful attention to your herds."*

Knowing the current stage of life for each of your oxen is important because it will govern how you use them. Here are phases of life you should expect:

a. **Baby Ox** Just as a baby ox is unable to withstand a full load, a fledgling business is usually not able to carry the burden a mature business can handle. This type of ox requires focused attention, but will grow up to carry a huge load in the future.

b. **Young Ox** A young ox is extremely energetic and can tend to run wildly at times. This is exactly what it feels like when you are the proud owner of a young business that is exploding! It is very exciting, but implementing controls is vital in order to keep the young business from running away.

c. **Healthy Strong Ox** This type of ox is very reliable. It has done its work for years on end, and it focuses on the task at hand. This ox can be counted upon for an abundant harvest with very little involvement.

d. **Aged and Weakening Ox** This is a natural stage of life for an ox. After delivering an abundant harvest for a long time, an ox will eventually weaken. A business or investment that is in this phase must be carefully monitored because a weakening ox can jeopardize your ability to produce an abundant harvest.

e. **Dead Ox** To state the very obvious, a dead ox cannot help you produce a harvest any longer (except maybe as fertilizer). It is always sad to have a business fail, but recognizing the situation and moving other oxen in to carry on the work is key to a continued abundant harvest.

In addition to knowing the current life stage of each of your oxen, you must know the current condition of each ox. For example, a healthy strong ox could fall ill for a brief period. Even though the sick ox is in its prime from an age standpoint, it won't be able to deliver like it normally can when fully healthy. Great businesses can experience challenges. These special conditions must be taken into account. Here are a few common conditions oxen experience that you must be vigilant to look for:

a. **Pregnant Ox** This occurs when a particular business is in the preparation stages of birthing a new product or service or launching a new business altogether. Just as it is important to take tremendous cautions in pregnancy, you should do the same when your business is preparing to give birth. For example, it is important to maintain substantial financial margin when launching a new product line because it helps ensure that the primary business is not jeopardized even if the new item fails.

Every time our organization prepares to launch a major initiative or new product, we pull back from all non-essential activities and spending in order to provide maximum support to our main business as well as the new baby ox. This has allowed our business to experience continued success even in cases where the baby ox did not make it.

b. **Injured/Sick Ox** Sometimes a business will experience a substantial and costly obstacle that could cause even a very healthy business to struggle. Many great businesses have been affected by sudden economic downturns that were far beyond their control. The businesses struggle through the tough economic time, but begin to prosper again as soon as the economy improves. Some businesses encounter legal challenges such as lawsuits that cause short term struggles.

Take care of your oxen when they encounter an injury or sickness reducing their performance for a period of time. If you do, they will recover to full strength and help you prosper.

c. **Stuck Ox** We've all seen businesses that become stuck. Blockbuster Video is a famous example of a stuck ox. While the entire video market converted to digital on-line delivery methods, they remained in bricks-and-mortar retail stores requiring people to drive to the store to rent a video. In this case, Blockbuster could not change swiftly enough and entered bankruptcy.[x] Always be on the lookout for potential pitfalls that could cause your business to become mired down, leading to the collapse and loss of your ox.

d. **Lost Ox** Sometimes oxen wander off and become lost. You might believe it is impossible to lose an ox, but it happens all of the time. In fact, you might have lost an ox yourself and do not even know it. A common lost ox is a retirement account or pension fund you established with a previous employer, but has somehow gotten lost in the shuffle and busyness of life. The ox may be continuing to perform work, but you won't receive the benefits of its labor until the ox is brought back to your herd.

Obviously, lost oxen provide zero opportunity for achieving an abundant harvest, so it is important to prevent them from wandering off. This is best accomplished by establishing clear boundaries and systems for each of your oxen. These clear "fences" will help you quickly determine if your ox is wandering away and allow you to redirect it back to its correct place. A great way to ensure that you do not lose oxen is to maintain a document that details each of your oxen and their individual value. I personally do this by preparing a net worth statement each and every month.

2. *Establish a Clear Measurement System*

One question will always stand above all others when it comes to owning oxen: **"Is this ox producing an abundant harvest?"** This is a very difficult question to answer if a clear and reliable measurement system is not in place. A clear measurement system will allow you to successfully lead and guide each of the oxen you are blessed to possess.

a. **Clear Financial Accounting and Record-Keeping** Excellent record-keeping is a hallmark of individuals who have achieved an abundant harvest. Without this in place, it is virtually impossible to understand exactly what is going on with each ox. Many people make the mistake of determining the success of their ox by only checking the daily balance of their bank account. This certainly provides a snapshot of its current status, but it provides little clarity regarding the actual revenue, costs, upcoming expenses, and necessary accruals.

At the very least, be certain to have a qualified person prepare financial statements for you to review every three months. These financial statements should include the "big three" reports:

i.   *Income Statements* An income statement reveals an ox's actual performance for a selected time period. It provides a summary of revenues received as well as expenses incurred. The real profit or loss of the business is the ultimate key figure provided by this report. For large businesses, income statements are generally prepared on a monthly basis. For smaller businesses, these reports are usually prepared on a quarterly basis.

ii. *Balance Sheet* A balance sheet provides a snapshot of the actual assets and liabilities an ox possesses at that very moment. A brief look will reveal short-term assets such as cash on hand and accounts receivable (invoices that customers have not yet paid), as well as long-term assets such as the value of property owned by the organization. This report details the current and long-term liabilities of the company. This can include short-term liabilities such as accounts payable (bills that are due) as well as long-term liabilities such as mortgage debt.

iii. *Statement of Cash Flows* This report shows the actual inflow and outflow of cash that has occurred during a specific time period. Because of the nature of financial accounting, an income statement can include accruals, depreciation, and various other items that might cloud the actual cash flow performance of the business. It has been famously said by many business people, "Cash flow is king!" This report allows you to clearly understand whether or not available cash is increasing or decreasing.

b. **Maintaining Separate Bank Accounts for Each Ox** Separate bank accounts for each ox is a great way to monitor performance. It prevents the potential of one ox's poor performance being masked by the excellent performance of another. Separate accounts provide clear documentation of the actual expenses and revenue for each ox, which is very helpful when selling them. An ox's past performance is able to be shown to the potential purchaser eliminating unnecessary confusion.

c. **Regular Financial Reviews and Audits** This is just a further admonishment to apply Proverbs 27:23 and, *"give careful attention to your herds."* Regular reviews and audits ensure you can have full faith and trust in your financial reports. This is exceptionally important since you will be using these reports to make major decisions as to the future use of each oxen. Regular reviews and audits allow you to operate with full integrity and character.

A clear measurement system is necessary for the ongoing management of your oxen. These metrics will vary by the type of business or investment you possess, but remember as you establish them that, "what gets measured, gets improved." Choose to focus on the top four or five items your oxen must do well, and implement an effective way to monitor them.

3. *Track Net Worth*

Net worth is the ultimate way to measure your harvest. Net worth is defined by Investopedia.com as, "the amount by which assets exceed liabilities."[xi] Put simply, your net worth is the amount of money that would remain if you sold everything you owned and satisfied all of your debts and financial obligations.

Let's look at an example to better understand this. Suppose a person named Tom has the following assets and liabilities.

Asset	Value	Liabilities	Amount Owed
House	175,000	Home Mortgage	160,000
Truck	21,000	Truck Debt	24,000
Car	17,000	Car Debt	19,500
Furnishings	1,800	Student Loan Debt	21,300
Bank Savings Account	200	Credit Card Debt	3,121
Total Assets	**215,000**	**Total Liabilities**	**227,921**
Net Worth			**-12,921**

Since Tom owes more than the value of everything he owns, he has a *negative* net worth of -$12,921. This does not mean Tom is bankrupt or a bad person. It simply means he has been living like the vast majority of people choose to live – week-to-week and broke-to-broke. Tom is 100 percent reliant on his income just to survive financially!

Let's say that Tom becomes tired of his situation and reads this book. He immediately realizes the importance of acquiring oxen and sets out to change his life, so he too, can experience an abundant harvest.

Tom starts a small business servicing swimming pools. He begins slowly as a side job and is soon able to secure a few dozen pool service contracts that pay him monthly. Tom prepares the contracts so that anyone who works for him can do the work. Over time, he is able to hire someone else to work with him. This provides Tom with more time to secure additional contracts. In just a few years, Tom's diligence is rewarded as the business grows to a value of $35,000.

He also births a Roth IRA ox and begins purchasing stocks, bonds, ETFs, and mutual funds within this retirement account. At the same time, Tom realizes the insanity of financing items that will not grow in value like vehicles, so he focused on paying off these debts. His efforts pay off as he becomes debt free except for his home.

By calculating his net worth, we can see the financial result of Tom's effort. His new net worth statement has changed substantially. The net result of Tom's mindset shift and oxen acquisition is a *positive* net worth of $123,500 instead of -$12,921. This is a total net worth change of $136,421 in just five years!

Asset	Value	Liabilities	Amount Owed
House	180,000	Home Mortgage	145,000
Truck	5,000	Truck Debt	0
Car	2,500	Car Debt	0
Furnishings	3,000	Student Loan Debt	0
Bank Savings Account	10,000	Credit Card Debt	0
Pool Servicing Business	35,000		
Roth IRA	33,000		
Total Assets	268,500	**Total Liabilities**	145,000
Net Worth			**123,500**

By now I'm sure you see there is incredible power in tracking your net worth. I encourage you to perform a net worth calculation at least once every three months. It will further demonstrate the strength of your oxen as this exercise reveals your abundant harvest. Net worth tracking is yet another way to put Proverbs 27:23 into practice as it allows you to *know* the condition of your flocks and herds.

I challenge you to take a moment right now to calculate your net worth on the form provided, or visit IWBNIN.com and find the on-line form via the "Tools" link. If you like what you see, congratulations! If you aren't too pleased, it's time to get some oxen!

Asset	Value		Liabilities	Amount Owed
Total Assets:			**Total Liabilities:**	
Net Worth				

4. *Maintain a Current and a Future Plan (Strategic and Financial)*

As I shared earlier, Proverbs 21:5 states, *"The plans of the diligent lead to profit; as surely as haste leads to poverty."* This is just as important for each of your oxen's financial health as it is for your personal financial health. You must have a plan for each ox. Knowing the status of your herd is great and having clear measurement systems in place is wonderful, but tracking net worth will tell you whether or not you are moving toward an abundant harvest. You can have each of these in place, but you will end up with oxen who perform poorly if you do not have a clear plan.

As you prepare your plan, here are some great questions to ask yourself and your team:

- What is your goal for each ox?
- How long do you want to keep each ox?
- Do you want to acquire more oxen in the future? If so, what type of oxen?
- Are any of your oxen going to be giving birth to a baby ox sometime in the future? If so, what steps are necessary to ensure its safe arrival and growth into a strong ox that helps produce an even larger harvest?
- Are any of your oxen facing major obstacles or hurdles? If so, what steps do you need to take to help restore them to full strength?
- In one year, what type of harvest do you expect?
- In five years, what type of harvest are you expecting?
- In 20 years, what type of harvest do you dream of?
- When you achieve an abundant harvest, how are you going to use it?

For those who have never owned financial oxen, the first steps can be quite intimidating. I've been there myself. If you need to borrow some belief, you can borrow it from me. I know you can do this. I believe in you. The very fact that you have read this much of this book tells me you are far above average in your interest in oxen ownership. It is my hope that you now have an anchor of confidence that allows you to take your next steps.

11

Leave a Legacy

Now that you have learned the value of oxen, how to acquire them, and how to lead them, it is now time to consider what you are going to do with the abundance. To manage the abundance in a way that honors God, your family, and blesses and helps those you love and those with tremendous needs, is perhaps the greatest challenge of all.

One key step toward maximizing your harvest is to continually invest in new oxen. The type of oxen you may acquire later in life may be different from those you possess now, but these investments will secure an abundant harvest for years into the future, perhaps even beyond your own life.

Proverbs 13:11 shares, *"Dishonest money dwindles away, but he who gathers little by little makes it grow."* Two key things can be learned from this verse. First, you must be certain to maintain your integrity as you gain oxen, or the harvest will dwindle away. After all, Proverbs 22:1 says, *"A good name is more desirable than great riches; to be esteemed is better than silver or gold."* The second key point in Proverbs 13:11 shows that when you gather money little by little, it will grow. This is wonderful news because we can all gather money *little by little*. I am so grateful it does not say *a lot by a lot*!

Make a commitment now to *always* invest. Always. It is what secures an ongoing abundant harvest that you will be able to use to bless so many others, as you live the rewarding life of generosity!

When you receive tremendous financial blessing, you are positioned to leave a legacy. It provides the opportunity to bless those currently around you as well as future generations. Proverbs 13:22 is a challenging verse for everyone: *"A good man leaves an inheritance for his children's children."* An abundant harvest allows you to fully meet this challenge! When I stop to consider the fact that I am positioning my children and grandchildren to prosper, it fires me up! I view this as a high honor and privilege.

It is very helpful to think through the potential use of an abundant harvest long before it is achieved. This can seem like an abstract idea if you do not yet have abundance, but the exercise can help provide direction throughout the process of birthing and acquiring oxen.

Use the following table to help clarify how you would like to leverage your future abundant harvest to leave a lasting legacy.

I want to give money to …	
I want to bless my spouse with …	
I want to bless my children with …	
I want to bless my parents with …	
I want to bless my friends with …	
I want to bless our employees with …	
I want to support these organizations …	
I want to bless complete strangers with …	
I want to purchase …	

Let me share a story of how one man used his abundant harvest to affect people in incredible ways, reaching far beyond the span of his own life. In the 1870's, a pharmacist named Eli Lilly began developing innovative prescription drugs. It has been said that his interest in new drug development was attributed to both the low quality drugs he was given during the Civil War and to the loss of his wife to malaria. [xii] His company, Eli Lilly and Company, grew rapidly and had direct involvement in treating some of the world's most terrible illnesses. The company was the first to mass produce penicillin which has been used to cure millions. In fact, most people alive today have benefitted from penicillin. The company was also the first to produce insulin on a large scale, and this brought incredible relief and healing to diabetics world-wide. The company developed the antibiotic known as erythromycin and the anti-depressants Prozac® and Cymbalta®. All of this great work led to a very profitable company. Throughout the history of the company, the leaders have focused on leaving a legacy.

In 1937, Eli's son and grandsons formed the Lilly Endowment, one of the largest private philanthropic organizations in the world. Eli Lilly and the Lilly Endowment are well known for *informed* philanthropy. They had an intentional plan to leave a legacy and make a huge impact on those who follow us on this ride around the sun. This organization has given incredible amounts of money to bless universities, cultural centers, community organizations, and religious groups. While they have given to causes around the world, the foundation has had intentional focus on giving back to those in its home state of Indiana because of the tremendous success the company has enjoyed there.

A story about a huge company that has given money away is not unusual. However, as a native of Indiana, I have been **personally affected** in multiple ways by their generosity. Purdue University, where my wife and I met and received our undergraduate education, was able to build their largest building on campus with money from the Lilly Endowment – the Lilly Hall of Life Sciences. A friend of mine was able to help fund his new church facility with funds provided by the Lilly Endowment. Franklin College, the local college near my hometown, was able to build new facilities because of money provided by the endowment. Lilly's support of the arts has impacted hundreds of thousands by helping to fund various museums and the living history museum, Conner Prairie.[xiii]

Generosity allows one to leave a tremendous legacy! The Lilly family leveraged their abundant harvest to bless many within their own generation as well as the generations that have followed. They have truly left a legacy.

While you might not achieve a harvest the size of the Lilly Endowment, you can impact many people with the harvest you do reap by applying the principles taught in this book.

My challenge to you is to obtain oxen, and use the abundant harvest to leave a tremendous legacy – for this generation and those who follow.

12

A Challenge

So there you have it. The word "oxen" will never mean the same to you again. With this book, I have given you my very best attempt at equipping you to achieve an abundant harvest.

Now it is time to set goals and establish deadlines. One of my favorite statements I regularly share is, "Thoughts and talk without action is mere babble." Here is my question for you: "What are you going to do with what you have learned?" Nothing will move until force is applied to it, just as acquiring oxen will not happen without action. Zig Ziglar, the world-renowned motivational expert, has famously said, "If you aim at nothing, you will hit it every time."

Let's start by gathering some of your thoughts and information that will be necessary to develop a great goal.

Where do you want to be in ten years?
• *Location?*
• *Family?*
• *Career?*
• *Travel?*
• *Other?*

What is your current net worth?

Now you can use this information to establish a goal that is SMART – **S**pecific, **M**easurable, **A**ttainable, **R**elevant, and **T**imebound.

Here's an example:

"In **10** years I want to own **3** oxen that are producing an abundant harvest of **$75,000** per year and possess a net worth of **$250,000**."

Now it is your turn to establish your goal:

In ____ years I want to own ____ oxen that are producing an abundant harvest of $_____ per year and possess a net worth of $_____.

Visit www.oxenbook.com and click on "Share Your Goal!" to share your dream with us. Our team will join you in praying for that goal!

I can't wait to hear your dream, and I really can't wait for the day that it becomes a reality. You can do this!

I have just one final question for you:

Got oxen?

I Was Broke. Now I'm Not.
(Book & Study Guide)

This book details how Joseph Sangl stopped being broke and started winning with money. He teaches how he became debt free in just 14 months and shares the tools that worked for him. In this entertaining and highly practical resource, you will be equipped to manage money in a way that allows you to fund your own dreams. You will learn how to plan your spending, calculate your debt freedom date, and calculate how much money you will need for retirement. You will also discover the power of compound interest and how investing captures that power allowing you to achieve true financial freedom.

A great way to learn these principles is through the *I Was Broke. Now I'm Not.* Group Study, a six week DVD-based small group study.

What Everyone Should Know About Money
Before They Enter The Real World
(Book & Study Guide)

There is a complete lack of financial training in today's schools. With this book, Joseph Sangl shares key financial tools and principles that are essential to winning with money. Topics include credit scores, planning for life, budgeting, giving, saving, debt, compound interest, insurance, and how money affects relationships. Help start a young person's life on the right track with this book!

Maximize the impact of this resource by obtaining the group study guide. It could be the most impactful six weeks of a young person's financial education!

www.IWBNIN.com

Footnotes

[i] According to Apple, Inc. company website http://investor.apple.com/faq.cfm

[ii] According to Yahoo! Finance for AAPL – http://finance.yahoo.com/echarts?s=AAPL+Interactive#symbol=aapl;range=my

[iii] According to The Billy Bob Teeth Company and http://billybobproducts.com/about-us.html

[iv] According to http://finance.yahoo.com/q/ks?s=HON+Key+Statistics as of 8/2/2012.

[v] According to http://www.quoteland.com/author/John-Wesley-Quotes/1000/

[vi] According to the book *Cheaper By The Dozen* by Frank B. Gilbreth, Jr. and Ernestine Gilbreth

[vii] Thomas Edison – GE Notes & History Page GE.com and according to http://www.ge.com/company/history/edison.html

[viii] According to Unilever's website - http://www.unilever.com/

[ix] Bill Gates - http://en.wikipedia.org/wiki/Bill_Gates and Microsoft Website - http://download.microsoft.com/download/1/3/0/130dd86a-a196-4700-b577-521c4cf5cec1/key_events_in_microsoft_history.doc

[x] According to http://en.wikipedia.org/wiki/Blockbuster_LLC

[xi] According to http://www.investopedia.com/terms/n/networth.asp#axzz1yug1UI00

[xii] Eli Lilly And Company according to http://en.wikipedia.org/wiki/Eli_Lilly_and_Company

[xiii] Conner Prairie according to http://en.wikipedia.org/wiki/Conner_Prairie